Simply the Best CHICKEN

RECIPES FROM GOLD KIST FARMS®

Bistro Chicken
Sandwich, page 83

Simply the Best CHICKEN

RECIPES FROM GOLD KIST FARMS

Barbara Davenport

Mega-Books

Editor: Barbara Bloch
Recipe Development: Barbara Gresak Davenport, Rosemary Dunn Stancil, Lorela Nichols Wilkins, Contest Winners
Editorial Management: Mary Pearce
Managing Editor, Production: Toni Ann Scaramuzzo
Editorial Assistance: John Krieger, Molly Walsh
Consulting Editor: Pat Fortunato
Photography: Phillip Vullo, Phillip Vullo Photography
Photography Art Director: Glenn Taylor, Mitchell Lindberg Inc.
Cover Photography Art Direction: Nancy Lycan, Lycomm Multi-Media
Food Stylist: Barbara Davenport, Gold Kist Inc.
Stylist's Assistant: Susan Strelecki
Prop Stylist: Jennifer Black Vullo
Design: How Bowers, Lycomm Multi-Media

Produced and published by Mega-Books, 240 East 60th Street, New York, NY 10022

Printed and bound in the United States of America
First Printing: October 1997

front cover: Plum Spicy Chicken, page 32;
back cover: Cornish Hens with Apple-Prune Stuffing, page 130

Table of CONTENTS

All Natural
GOLD KIST
FARMS®
Young'n Tender®
Chicken

Introduction

Everyone who cooks loves passing along recipes to friends, a simple act that brings comfort and pleasure to those we care about. At Gold Kist, sharing information has always been part of our heritage, with farm families handing down their knowledge of raising chickens from generation to generation. And from the time we decided to put our brand name on our products, we have made it a point to pass along great recipes and information about the preparation of chicken.

It's always been a pleasure to share our original recipes, which are developed by professional home economists either in our own Gold Kist kitchen or under our direct supervision. In 1989, we added another dimension — the participation of our consumers. "The Winning Taste Recipe Contest®" helps us maintain a meaningful dialogue with our customers. We learn about the ways they prepare and serve chicken, how they are changing the way they cook, the cultures that are influencing their choices, and the special ingredients they like to use. Every year, we are amazed by the huge volume of entries and by the wide variety of new ideas consumers have created with America's favorite, most healthy, and versatile meat.

Selecting the winning recipes is a very difficult task, which is assigned to a team of food professionals. Each entry is read and discussed in detail until the final contenders are named. These recipes are tested for accuracy by home economists and judged on originality, appearance, ease of preparation, and above all, taste. Once winners are selected and notified, the recipes are tested again, rewritten for clarity and photographed to appear in booklets which we distribute to our customers.

For many years, it has been our dream to publish a full-length Gold Kist chicken cookbook, and finally it is a reality. *Simply the Best Chicken* is by no means a complete collection of all of our recipes; it's just a taste. But we believe it will satisfy the many requests we've had for up-to-date and practical recipes that go beyond traditional favorites such as Southern Fried Chicken to include the grilled, marinated, skewered, fancy-filled breasts, fajitas, pizzas, and stir-frys of today.

Our goal is to provide delicious solutions to mealtime gatherings, based on our own research and the shared experiences of our friends across the country. We hope that this book will become a trusted resource for you and your family, and that when you choose a recipe from *Simply The Best Chicken*, you'll use simply the best chicken — from Gold Kist Farms.

Barbara Davenport

Marketing Manager

GOLD KIST INC.
A FARMER-OWNED COMPANY

The story of Gold Kist began in 1933 in the depths of the Great Depression. A farmer's annual income was said to be only $72 per year, and cotton, the predominant crop, was selling for only a nickel a pound. Several unsuccessful attempts had been made at starting a farm cooperative in the largest cotton producing county in Georgia. Undaunted, a young agronomy instructor at the University of Georgia, learned from the mistakes of his predecessors and took up the challenge of organizing still another farm cooperative in Carroll County, Georgia. Financed with a $2,100 unsecured loan from a local bank, D.W. Brooks, son of a merchant in Royston, GA, and 13 area cotton farmers formed Cotton Producers Association, which later became Gold Kist. The organization made it through one year, then another. The rest, as they say, is history.

Gold Kist has become one of the nation's largest farm cooperatives with more than $2 billion in annual sales. Headquartered in Atlanta, GA, it is owned by more than 50,000 farmer-members whose farms lie from South Carolina to Texas. Gold Kist employs nearly 20,000 people at more than 200 locations in 16 states.

Gold Kist entered the poultry business by selling feed and operating a hatchery to provide chicks to growers in Gainsville, Georgia.

Begun as a cotton marketing cooperative, Gold Kist has diversified through the years. Its operations touch almost every facet of agriculture. Soon after its founding, the cooperative purchased a fertilizer plant to get members better fertilizer at lower prices, and then it expanded into animal feeds. In 1944, Gold Kist opened is first farm supply store in Statesboro, GA. Today, more than 100 Gold Kist Stores supply commercial farmers with fertilizer, crop protection chemicals, seed, feed and other products and services.

In addition to these agricultural endeavors, Gold Kist is also a major pork producer and is involved in cotton ginning, warehousing and marketing; the manufacture of pet foods; aquaculture research; plant breeding and genetics; peanut and pecan processing; and agricultural financing.

GOLD KIST POULTRY OPERATIONS

It was through its farm supply store in Gainesville, GA, that Gold Kist entered the poultry industry in the 1940s. The store sold feed to chicken producers. As a service to these members, it began operating a hatchery and sold baby chicks to producers. Gold Kist saw a need to assist its members who were suffering economically because of the system's inefficiency. It also saw the poultry industry as a viable business opportunity if order and efficiency could be brought to the chaotic operations through vertical integration.

A group of cotton farmers from Carrollton, Georgia, pooled their cotton to get better prices, and Gold Kist was formed.

Gold Kist field representatives, like Jimmy Dean Green, provide technical advice to the growers.

Integration unifies most of the components of poultry production under one management system. Controlling the entire process of providing chickens to consumers, including the hatchery, growout operations, feed mills, processing plant and marketing and distribution activities, assures maximum efficiency and total quality control.

In 1951, Gold Kist took the first step to become a fully integrated poultry processor by acquiring its first processing plant in Holly Springs, GA. This first plant processed about 60,000 broilers per week — now an average plant processes 1.2 million per week.

Today, Gold Kist is the second largest poultry processor in the United States operating 10 fully integrated poultry divisions in the Southeast. To ensure maximum efficiency and quality control, each division operates its own hatcheries, feed mill, processing plant, marketing and distribution activities.

Gold Kist delivers chicks from its hatcheries to its broiler grower members who raise the chicks to market weight. During growout, Gold Kist provides high quality feed for the birds, veterinary services and other technical expertise on raising the birds. The grower-member provides the houses, electricity and the day-to-day attention to nurture and care for the birds. "I never let a chicken leave here that I wouldn't eat myself," said Jack Nally, a Gold Kist director and grower-member, about his insistence on quality at the farm level.

When market weight is reached, the company processes the birds — more than 14 million per week. Gold Kist maintains strict product quality standards for all products produced at its processing plants. Gold Kist products pass through approximately 96 quality control points before being packaged for customers. Company standards exceed, and in most cases, are much tougher than those imposed by the federal government.

Gold Kist sells its products to retail, institutional and fast food customers and exports product to many foreign countries. Its retail lines, sold under the Gold Kist Farms brand name, include fresh and frozen cut up products, deboned and skinless products, Cornish Hens, and many further processed products.

Gold Kist is a highly diversified company dedicated to helping its farmer-members deliver high quality agricultural products and the finest, freshest chicken anywhere to consumers in the United States and around the world.

Gold Kist member and director Jack Nally and wife Jewell provide the daily care to produce top quality Gold Kist Farms brand chicken.

D. W. BROOKS

A COMMITMENT TO AGRICULTURE

D. W. BROOKS, THE FOUNDER OF GOLD KIST INC., has devoted his life to improving agriculture and the economic well-being of farmers. Brooks rose from a country farmer to an agribusiness giant by way of hard work, education and vision. His commitment to improve farm income is the ideal on which Gold Kist was founded and remains the backbone of the company to this day.

In a time when many men were leaving the farm to pursue careers that yielded higher financial rewards, Brooks chose to attend the College of Agriculture at the University of Georgia. He obtained his masters degree and began teaching agronomy.

In the early 1930s, Brooks left the University to form a cooperative to improve conditions for Georgia farmers. Brooks and thirteen area farmers started Cotton Producers Association which later became Gold Kist Inc. Brooks served as general manager of Gold Kist from its inception until 1968 when he became chairman of the board. In 1977, he retired and was named chairman of the board emeritus.

Brooks's knowledge and wisdom has helped many people — from peasant farmers in Russia and China to world leaders. An advisor to seven presidents, he has served on agricultural commissions, committees for trade negotiations, commissions on rural poverty, and the presidential commission on world hunger. In recent years, he has served as a visiting professor at the University of Georgia, making him the oldest teaching professor.

Harold Martin's 1982 biography of Brooks states, "It was his [Brooks's] dream of what the wise and willing farmer could produce...which inspired him to create, out of the little Georgia Cotton Producers Association of the 1930s, the globe girding agricultural production, marketing and purchasing cooperative that is Gold Kist today." Gold Kist, a diversified agribusiness, is now one of the largest farm cooperatives and the second largest poultry processor in the United States.

❖ ❖ ❖ ❖

A cookbook from a company founded in the South would not be complete without a recipe for fried chicken. D. W. Brooks's favorite recipe happens to be Oven-Fried Chicken.

Brooks Family Oven-Fried Chicken

Preheat oven to 350°F. Melt 1/4 cup (1/2 stick) butter or margarine in baking pan and set aside. Cut up 3 1/2 to 4 pound Gold Kist Farms whole chicken into serving pieces, rinse, pat dry, and season with salt. Dredge chicken in all-purpose flour to coat all sides and place in prepared baking pan. Bake in preheated oven 1 hour, turning after 30 minutes, until chicken is fork-tender and juices run clear when thighs are pierced with fork. Remove chicken with tongs, drain on paper towels and place on serving platter. 4 to 6 servings.

Singapore Chicken Skewers, page 19

Chicken Quesadillas

INGREDIENTS

- 2 tablespoons butter or margarine
- 1 tablespoon olive or vegetable oil
- 3 to 4 *Gold Kist Farms* boneless, skinless, split chicken breasts (about 2 pounds), chopped
- 1 cup chopped broccoli
- ½ pound fresh mushrooms, sliced
- 2 cloves garlic, minced
- 1 jar (4 ounces) mild green chilies, drained and chopped
- 1 teaspoon ground cumin
- Salt to taste
- 8 flour tortillas (8-inch size)
- 2½ cups (10 ounces) shredded Cheddar or taco-seasoned cheese, divided
- ½ cup thinly sliced scallions (green onions)
- 1 small red bell pepper, chopped
- Picante sauce to serve (optional)

Preheat oven to 350°F. Lightly grease 2 baking sheets and set aside.

Melt butter with oil in large skillet. Add chicken and stir-fry until no longer pink inside. Remove chicken from skillet with slotted spoon and set aside.

Place broccoli in skillet and stir-fry about 5 minutes. Add mushrooms and garlic to skillet and stir-fry until mushrooms are softened. Add chilies, cumin, and salt. Cook just until all ingredients are heated through.

Place 4 tortillas on prepared baking sheets. Layer chicken, vegetables, and 1¾ cups of cheese on tortillas, dividing ingredients equally. Top with remaining 4 tortillas and sprinkle with remaining ¾ cup cheese, scallions, and red pepper.

Bake in preheated oven 10 to 12 minutes or until cheese is melted. Cut each quesadilla into 4 wedges and serve immediately with picante sauce on the side, if desired.

16 wedges

Chicken Bayou Petites

INGREDIENTS

- 1 tablespoon butter or margarine
- 1 tablespoon olive or vegetable oil
- 3 to 4 *Gold Kist Farms* boneless, skinless, split chicken breasts (about 2 pounds), chopped
- ½ cup chopped onion
- 1 can (8 ounces) stewed tomatoes, chopped, liquid reserved
- ¼ cup minced red bell pepper
- 1 large clove garlic, minced
- ¼ teaspoon hot pepper sauce
- 1 teaspoon salt or to taste
- 2 cans (11½ ounces each) refrigerated corn bread twist dough (see Note)
- ⅔ cup dairy sour cream
- 1 tablespoon honey
- ½ teaspoon paprika

Note: Refrigerated corn bread twist dough can be found in dairy section of supermarket.

Preheat oven to 350° F. Spray with cooking spray or lightly grease sixteen 3 × 1¼-inch muffin pan cups and set aside.

Melt butter with oil in large skillet. Add chicken and onion. Stir-fry about 3 minutes or until onion is transparent. Stir in tomatoes with liquid, red pepper, garlic, hot pepper sauce, and salt. Cook about 2 minutes or until chicken is no longer pink inside. Set aside to cool while preparing corn bread cups.

Unroll 1 can of corn bread dough and divide into eight 2-strip portions. Press 2 strips together to join at seam and cut double strip in half crosswise. Place halves together to form square and press to join at seam. Press square into muffin cup. Repeat with remaining seven 2-strip portions. Repeat with second can of corn bread dough.

Place sour cream in bowl and stir in honey. Add to chicken mixture and stir to combine. Spoon mixture into corn bread cups, filling ⅔ full. Sprinkle with paprika.

Bake in preheated oven 20 minutes or until filling is set and corn bread cups are lightly browned. Remove from oven and serve immediately.

16 appetizers

Spicy Potato Chip-Chicken Sticks

INGREDIENTS

- 3 heads garlic, cloves separated and peeled
- 1 cup extra light olive oil
- 1/4 teaspoon hot pepper sauce or to taste
- 1 1/2 cups crushed plain or flavored potato chips
- 3 to 4 *Gold Kist Farms* boneless, skinless, split chicken breasts (about 2 pounds), cut into 1-inch strips

DIPPING SAUCE

- 1/2 cup Dijon-style mustard
- 1/2 cup German-style mustard
- 1 tablespoon Chinese-style mustard
- 1/3 cup honey
- 1/3 cup light cream
- 1/4 cup mayonnaise

Preheat oven to 375°F.

Place garlic, oil, and hot pepper sauce in blender or food processor and process until smooth. Transfer to bowl. Place crushed potato chips in separate bowl. Dip chicken strips in garlic mixture, then in chips. Place coated strips in single layer in shallow baking pan. Drizzle remaining garlic mixture over chicken and sprinkle with remaining chips. Bake 15 to 20 minutes or until chicken is brown, crispy, and no longer pink inside. Place on serving dish.

To make sauce, place mustards, honey, and cream in small bowl. Beat with whisk until well combined. Add mayonnaise and beat well. Place in serving bowl.

To serve, place bowl of mustard sauce in center of serving dish and surround with chicken sticks.

6 to 8 servings

▲ Spicy Potato Chip-Chicken Sticks, facing page

▼ Greek Marinated Chicken, page 18

Greek Marinated Chicken with Feta Cheese

INGREDIENTS

3 to 4 *Gold Kist Farms* boneless, skinless, split chicken breasts (about 2 pounds)
2/3 cup dry white wine

MARINADE

1/4 cup olive oil
3 tablespoons red wine vinegar
3 tablespoons drained capers
1 tablespoon lemon juice (juice of about 1/4 lemon)
1 teaspoon dried oregano
1 teaspoon freshly ground pepper
1 clove garlic, crushed

❖ ❖ ❖ ❖

Feta or chèvre cheese, cut into 1/2-inch cubes
Black olives
Hot crusty bread to serve

Place chicken in single layer in large saucepan, add white wine and 1/3 cup water. Bring to a boil, reduce heat to simmer, cover, and poach 12 to 15 minutes or until chicken is no longer pink inside. Drain and set aside to cool.

To make marinade, place oil, vinegar, capers, lemon juice, oregano, pepper, and garlic in 2-cup measuring cup and beat with whisk until well combined.

When chicken has cooled, cut into 1-inch strips, and place strips in single layer in non-metallic dish or resealable plastic bag. Pour marinade over chicken, cover or close bag, and refrigerate at least 1 hour.

Remove chicken from marinade with slotted spoon and place on 8 individual plates with cheese and olives. Serve with bread.

8 appetizer servings

Singapore Chicken Skewers

INGREDIENTS

- 3 to 4 *Gold Kist Farms* boneless, skinless, split chicken breasts (about 2 pounds), cut into 1-inch cubes
- 3 red bell peppers, cut into bite-size pieces
- 1 package (8 ounces) pitted dates, halved

MARINADE

- 1/4 cup balsamic vinegar
- 2 tablespoons peanut oil
- 1 tablespoon teriyaki sauce
- 1 1/2 teaspoons sesame oil
- 2 teaspoons brown sugar
- 1 1/2 teaspoons grated fresh ginger or 1/2 teaspoon ground ginger
- 1 teaspoon minced garlic
- 1/2 teaspoon crushed cumin seed
- 1/2 teaspoon cayenne, or to taste
- 1/4 teaspoon liquid smoke (optional)

Note: Sesame oil and teriyaki sauce can be found in Asian food stores or in Asian section of supermarket.

Place chicken, peppers, and dates in large non-metallic bowl or large resealable plastic bag and set aside.

To make marinade, place marinade ingredients in small bowl and beat with whisk until well combined. Pour over chicken mixture and toss to coat. Cover or close bag and refrigerate at least 1 hour or overnight.

Soak approximately forty-eight 6-inch wooden skewers in water 15 minutes, remove from water, and set aside. Preheat grill and lightly coat with oil or cooking spray.

Remove chicken, peppers, and dates from marinade with slotted spoon and set aside. Pour marinade into small saucepan and bring to a boil. Reduce heat and simmer 5 minutes, stirring occasionally.

Thread chicken, peppers, and dates alternately on skewers. Place filled skewers on prepared grill about 4 to 6 inches from source of heat. Cook, turning frequently and basting with cooked marinade, about 15 to 18 minutes or until chicken is no longer pink inside.

48 skewers

Fiesta Chicken Party Roll

INGREDIENTS

3 to 4 *Gold Kist Farms* boneless, skinless, split chicken breasts (about 2 pounds)
⅔ cup thick salsa, mild or medium
3 tablespoons thinly sliced scallions (green onions)
3 tablespoons chopped fresh cilantro
3 tablespoons chopped red bell pepper
½ teaspoon chili powder
1 teaspoon lime juice
½ cup (2 ounces) shredded Cheddar or taco-seasoned cheese
⅓ cup mayonnaise
1 cup chopped pecans (optional)
Crackers to serve

Place chicken in single layer in large saucepan. Add enough water to cover by ½ inch. Bring to a boil, reduce heat to simmer, cover, and poach 12 to 15 minutes or until chicken is no longer pink inside. Drain and set aside until cool enough to handle. Dice chicken and place in large bowl. Stir in remaining ingredients except pecans and crackers. Mix thoroughly.

Place about 8-inch length of aluminum foil on flat surface. Spoon chicken mixture down center of long (12-inch) length of foil. Form chicken mixture into 10-inch log. Sprinkle exposed surface of log with pecans, if desired, and pat gently. Lift edge of foil and roll log over. Cover newly exposed surface of log with pecans, if desired. Close foil around log, place on dish, and refrigerate overnight.

To serve, remove foil, place on serving dish, and surround with crackers.

10-inch roll

MexaMia Chicken Puffs

INGREDIENTS

3 to 4 *Gold Kist Farms* boneless, skinless, split chicken breasts (about 2 pounds)
10 slices (each about ½-inch thick) white or sourdough bread, crusts removed
1 cup (4 ounces) shredded mild Cheddar cheese
1 cup (4 ounces) shredded Monterey Jack cheese
1 cup (4 ounces) shredded mozzarella cheese
1 jar (16 ounces) picante sauce
2 scallions (green onions), thinly sliced, green tops included
1 clove garlic, minced
1 can (15 ounces) black beans, drained and rinsed
¼ cup (about 1 ounce) diced pepperoni
4 eggs, lightly beaten
2¼ cups milk
1 can (4 ounces) diced green chilies, undrained
¼ teaspoon ground cumin
⅛ teaspoon chili powder
Salt and freshly ground pepper to taste
Dairy sour cream to serve (optional)
Sliced black olives for garnish (optional)

Place chicken in single layer in large saucepan. Add enough water to cover by ½ inch. Bring to a boil, reduce heat to simmer, cover, and poach 12 to 15 minutes or until chicken is no longer pink inside. Drain, set aside to cool, chop, and set aside.

Line bottom of 13 × 9 × 2-inch baking dish with 5 slices of bread. Combine cheeses in large bowl and sprinkle half of mixture over bread. Place picante sauce in bowl and stir in scallions and garlic. Pour half of mixture over cheese. Top with half the chicken and half the black beans. Sprinkle top evenly with all of pepperoni.

Repeat layers beginning with remaining 5 bread slices, and ending with beans. Place eggs in bowl, add milk, and beat to combine. Stir in chilies, cumin, chili powder, salt, and pepper. Pour evenly over top. Cover and refrigerate 4 hours or overnight.

Preheat oven to 350°F.

Bake in preheated oven 55 minutes or until set. Allow to sit about 30 minutes before serving. Cut into 2 × 1-inch rectangles. Top each serving with dollop of sour cream and garnish with olive slices, if desired.

54 appetizers

Note: This is also delicious when served as a casserole. Eliminate standing time, garnish as above, and serve immediately.
6 to 8 servings as main dish casserole

Tex-Mex Chicken Cups

INGREDIENTS

2 to 3 *Gold Kist Farms* boneless, skinless, split chicken breasts (about 1½ pounds)
1 cup ranch-style dressing or dairy sour cream
Salt and freshly ground pepper to taste
2 cups (8 ounces) shredded Monterey Jack cheese
2 tablespoons chili seasoning blend or 4 teaspoons chili powder and 2 teaspoons paprika
1 package (24) wonton wrappers
1 cup diced red and/or green bell pepper
Salsa, dairy sour cream, and guacamole to serve (optional)

Note: To make minicups, use 1¾ x 1-inch muffin cups. Use same size wonton wrapper and fill each cup with scant tablespoon or 2 teaspoons filling. Bake about 5 minutes, or until filling is heated through and cheese is melted. About 48 minicups

Preheat oven to 350°F. Spray with cooking spray or lightly grease twenty-four 2½ × 1-inch muffin pan cups.

Place chicken in single layer in large saucepan and add enough water to cover by ½ inch. Bring to a boil, reduce heat to simmer, cover, and poach 12 to 15 minutes or until chicken is no longer pink inside. Drain and set aside until cool enough to handle.

Shred chicken and place in bowl. Stir in dressing and season with salt and pepper. Set aside. Combine cheese and chili seasoning blend in medium-size bowl and set aside.

Place 1 wonton wrapper in each prepared muffin cup and bake in preheated oven 5 minutes or until lightly browned. Remove from oven and set aside 2 to 3 minutes to crisp. (Do not turn oven off.) Spoon heaping tablespoon chicken filling into each wonton cup and sprinkle with reserved cheese mixture. Top with bell pepper. Return to oven and bake 5 to 10 minutes or until filling is heated through and cheese is melted.

To serve, top with salsa, sour cream, and guacamole, or serve on the side, if desired.

24 wonton cups

▲ Tex-Mex Chicken Cups, facing page

▼ Spicy Chinese Chicken Wings, page 24

Spicy Chinese Chicken Wings

INGREDIENTS

16 to 24 *Gold Kist Farms* chicken wings, cut at joints, wing tips discarded

MARINADE

1 jar (9 ounces) hoisin sauce (see Note)
¼ cup firmly packed brown sugar
3 tablespoons soy sauce
2 teaspoons chili paste (see Note)
¼ teaspoon minced garlic

Note: Hoisin sauce and chili paste can be found in Asian food section of supermarket. If chili paste is unavailable, substitute 1 teaspoon crushed red pepper or to taste.

Place chicken wing sections in large non-metallic bowl or large resealable plastic bag and set aside.

To make marinade, place hoisin sauce, brown sugar, soy sauce, chili paste, and garlic in bowl. Beat with whisk until well combined. Pour ⅔ of marinade over wings and toss to coat. Reserve remaining marinade for basting. Cover or close bag and refrigerate at least 1 hour or overnight.

Preheat oven to 425° F. Lightly coat broiler pan with oil or cooking spray. Remove wings from marinade and discard marinade (do not use for basting).

Place wings on broiler pan in single layer and bake in preheated oven 10 minutes. Baste wings with reserved (unused) marinade, turn, baste, and bake 10 to 15 minutes.

32 to 48 appetizers

Chicken-Cheese Pizza Bread

INGREDIENTS

- 4 tablespoons olive oil, divided
- ¾ pound *Gold Kist Farms* boneless, skinless, split chicken breasts or thighs, ground (see Note)
- 1 teaspoon dried basil
- ½ teaspoon dried oregano
- Salt and freshly ground pepper to taste
- 1 medium-size onion, chopped
- 2 cloves garlic, minced
- 1 package (10 ounces) refrigerated pizza crust dough
- 2½ cups (10 ounces) shredded mozzarella cheese

Note: Grind chicken in food processor or blender or have butcher grind for you at supermarket.

Preheat oven to 350°F. Grease baking sheet and set aside.

Heat 2 tablespoons oil in large skillet and cook ground chicken, stirring, until chicken is no longer pink. Stir in basil, oregano, salt, and pepper. Remove chicken with slotted spoon and set aside. Wipe out skillet.

Heat remaining 2 tablespoons oil in skillet. Add onion and cook until transparent. Add garlic and cook 2 minutes. Stir into chicken and set aside.

Roll out pizza dough on lightly floured surface to 8 × 11-inch rectangle. Spread chicken mixture over dough to within ½ inch of edges and sprinkle top with cheese.

Starting at narrow end, roll up jelly-roll style and place, seam-side down, on prepared baking sheet. Pinch ends of roll together to seal. Bake in preheated oven 20 to 30 minutes or until golden brown.

To serve, cut into 1-inch slices or cut each slice into quarters.

Eight 1-inch slices for snacks or 32 bite-size pieces for appetizers

Chicken-Broccoli Triangles

INGREDIENTS

- 2 tablespoons vegetable or olive oil
- 1½ pounds *Gold Kist Farms* boneless, skinless chicken thighs, ground (see Note)
- ¼ teaspoon crushed red pepper
- 1 clove garlic, minced
- 1 package (10 ounces) frozen chopped broccoli, thawed, patted dry, and minced
- 1 can (10¾ ounces) condensed cream of chicken-mushroom soup, undiluted
- ¾ cup grated Parmesan cheese
- ½ cup chopped fresh cilantro
- 12 phyllo leaves (approximately half of 16-ounce box), thawed if frozen (see Note)
- 1¼ cups (2½ sticks) butter, melted (no substitution)

Note: Grind chicken in food processor or blender or have butcher grind for you at supermarket.
Phyllo leaves are sold in 16-ounce boxes, approximately 22 leaves per box, each leaf about 14 x 18 inches. Frozen dough should be thawed in refrigerator. If defrosted at room temperature, leaves will stick together. Unbaked, filled triangles may be frozen in single layers and then stored up to 1 month in covered containers, layers separated by wax paper. When frozen before baking, let stand at room temperature 10 minutes before baking.

Heat oil in large skillet. Add chicken, red pepper, and garlic. Cook, stirring, about 5 minutes or until chicken is no longer pink. Remove with slotted spoon and place in large bowl. Add broccoli, soup, cheese, and cilantro. Stir to combine well, cover, and place in refrigerator to chill about 1 hour or until mixture holds together.

Lightly grease 1 or more large baking sheets and set aside.

Remove 12 phyllo leaves from package and unfold on flat, dry surface. Stack leaves and cut stack into seven 2-inch wide strips to make 84 strips, each 2 × 18 inches. Remove 1 strip and cover remaining strips with damp kitchen towel or plastic wrap. Brush single strip lightly with melted butter, covering entire surface including edges. Place 1 heaping teaspoonful filling about ½ inch from bottom of strip. Pick up corner of strip at right bottom edge and fold toward left side of strip over filling to make triangle. Pick up point of triangle and fold straight up, making fold at bottom edge of triangle. Continue folding, flag-style, folding over to right side of strip, then straight up, and then to left side. Brush with butter and place, seam-side down, on prepared baking sheet. Brush top with butter. Repeat with remaining strips.

Preheat oven to 375°F about 10 to 15 minutes before last triangle has been made. Bake 1 or 2 filled baking sheets at a time in preheated oven 15 to 20 minutes or until golden brown. Remove from baking sheets and serve hot or cold.

84 triangles or appetizers

Variation: To make richer pastry, wrap filling in double strip of dough. To make larger triangles, cut leaves into four 3½ inch wide strips and increase filling by about ½ teaspoon.

Chicken-Broccoli Triangles, facing page

Cornish Luxembourg Fans

INGREDIENTS

4 *Gold Kist Farms* Cornish Hens (1 pound 6 ounces each)

STUFFING

1 tablespoon butter or margarine
½ pound fresh mushrooms, minced
5 scallions (green onions), minced, green tops included
1 clove garlic, minced
¼ cup plus 3 tablespoons Madeira, divided
1 tablespoon minced fresh sage, or ½ teaspoon dried sage
Salt and white pepper to taste

Remove giblets and cut off wings. Reserve for use another time. Rinse hens and pat dry. Cut off drumsticks and thighs, leave breasts whole. Crack breast bones so breasts lie flat. Set aside.

To make stuffing, remove meat and skin from drumsticks and thighs. Discard skin and bones and place meat in blender or food processor. Process until fine paste is formed and set aside.

Melt butter in large skillet and sauté mushrooms and scallions about 4 minutes. Add garlic and cook 3 minutes. Add 3 tablespoons Madeira and cook 2 to 3 minutes until reduced slightly. Remove from heat and set aside to cool 5 minutes. Add meat paste, sage, salt, and pepper. Stir to combine.

Preheat oven to 350° F.

Place whole breasts, skin-side up, on flat work surface. Divide stuffing into 4 portions and spread evenly between breast meat and skin of each breast. Place stuffed breasts in single layer, skin-side up, in large baking pan and bake in preheated oven 25 to 30 minutes or until juices run clear when breast meat is pierced with fork.

Remove breasts from baking pan and let stand 5 minutes. Pour remaining ¼ cup Madeira into baking pan and stir over heat, scraping up drippings. Set sauce aside. Gently pull breast meat away from bones and cut whole breasts in half. Carefully slice each breast half into ¼-inch slices.

To serve, spoon sauce evenly on 8 serving plates. Place slices from 1 split breast in fan shape over sauce. Repeat with each serving.

8 appetizer servings, 4 main dish servings

Cornish Luxembourg
Fans, facing page

Main Dishes

Italian Chicken, page 33

Plum Spicy Chicken

INGREDIENTS

- ¼ cup all-purpose flour
- 2 teaspoons ground ginger
- ⅛ teaspoon garlic powder
- ½ teaspoon cayenne
- Salt to taste
- 2 tablespoons vegetable oil
- 4 *Gold Kist Farms* boneless, skinless, split chicken breasts
- 1 jar (8 ounces) plum sauce (see Note)
- ¼ cup Chinese-style mustard
- 2 tablespoons sesame seed, toasted to garnish
- 1 scallion (green onion), thinly sliced, green top included to garnish

Note: Plum sauce may be found in Asian food stores or in Asian food section of supermarket.

Place flour, ginger, garlic, cayenne, and salt in pie plate and stir to combine. Coat chicken lightly.

Heat oil in large skillet over medium heat. Add chicken and sauté 5 to 10 minutes on each side or until lightly browned and no longer pink inside. Remove chicken with spatula, place on serving platter, and keep warm.

Place plum sauce and mustard in small saucepan and cook over medium heat until heated through. Brush over chicken generously and sprinkle with sesame seed and scallion.

4 servings

Italian Chicken

INGREDIENTS

- 4 *Gold Kist Farms* boneless, skinless, split chicken breasts
- ¼ pound sweet Italian sausage
- 1 large onion, thinly sliced
- ½ cup sliced celery
- ½ cup chopped green pepper
- ½ cup chopped red pepper
- ¼ cup chopped carrots
- 1 can (8 ounces) sliced mushrooms, drained
- 1 can (16 ounces) tomatoes, cut into quarters, liquid reserved
- 1 can (8 ounces) tomato sauce
- 2 bay leaves
- 1 teaspoon dried basil
- 1 teaspoon dried oregano
- 2 tablespoons grated Parmesan cheese
- 1 clove garlic, minced
- Salt and freshly ground pepper to taste
- ½ cup (2 ounces) shredded mozzarella cheese
- 8 ounces (half of 16-ounce package) hot, cooked angel hair pasta

Place chicken breasts in single layer in baking pan and set aside.

Preheat oven to 350° F.

Brown sausage in large skillet, stirring to crumble. Remove with slotted spoon and discard all but 2 tablespoons fat. Add onion, celery, green and red peppers, and carrots to skillet. Cook just until vegetables are fork-tender, but not browned. Drain excess fat. Add mushrooms, tomatoes with juice, tomato sauce, bay leaves, basil, oregano, Parmesan cheese, garlic, salt, pepper, and cooked sausage. Stir to combine with vegetables and spoon over chicken breasts.

Cover and bake in preheated oven 45 minutes. Remove and discard bay leaves. Sprinkle mozzarella cheese over chicken and bake, uncovered, 5 to 10 minutes or just until cheese is melted.

To serve, spoon pasta on 4 dinner plates and top each serving with chicken breast and sauce. Serve immediately.

4 servings

Peppery Pecan Chicken

INGREDIENTS

- 4 *Gold Kist Farms* boneless, skinless, split chicken breasts
- 1/4 cup all-purpose flour
- 1/4 cup minced pecans
- 1 1/2 teaspoons lemon-pepper seasoning
- 1/2 teaspoon salt or to taste
- 3/4 cup honey
- 1 tablespoon chopped fresh rosemary or 1 teaspoon dried rosemary
- 1 1/2 teaspoons freshly ground pepper or to taste
- 3 tablespoons vegetable oil
- Lemon slices and rosemary sprigs to garnish (optional)
- Hot baking powder biscuits to serve

Rinse chicken and pat dry. Set aside. Place flour, pecans, lemon-pepper seasoning, and salt in shallow dish. Stir to combine and set aside.

Place honey, 1/3 cup water, rosemary, and pepper in small saucepan. Simmer, swirling sauce in pan occasionally, until reduced to about 3/4 cup. Pour half of sauce into shallow dish and set aside to cool. Leave remaining sauce in saucepan and set aside for later use. Dip chicken in cooled sauce in shallow dish, then dip in reserved flour mixture to coat lightly on all sides.

Heat oil in large skillet over medium heat. Add chicken breasts and cook about 6 minutes on each side or until browned on both sides and no longer pink inside. Watch carefully to prevent burning.

To serve, place chicken on warm serving platter. Reheat sauce remaining in saucepan and drizzle over chicken. Garnish with lemon slices and fresh rosemary, if desired, and serve with baking powder biscuits.

4 servings

▲ Peppery Pecan Chicken, facing page

▼ Chicken Symphonic, page 36

Chicken Symphonic

INGREDIENTS

- 1/3 cup butter or margarine, melted
- 1/4 cup thinly sliced scallions (green onions), green tops included
- 1/4 cup sliced smoked almonds (see Note)
- 1/4 cup all-purpose flour
- 2 tablespoons sesame seed, toasted
- 1/2 teaspoon garlic powder
- 1 teaspoon salt or to taste
- Freshly ground pepper to taste
- 4 *Gold Kist Farms* boneless, skinless, split chicken breasts

SAUCE

- 1 cup dairy sour cream
- 2 tablespoons prepared horseradish
- 2 teaspoons milk
- 2 tablespoons chopped fresh parsley
- 2 tablespoons sliced, smoked almonds

Variation: If smoked almonds are not available, combine 6 tablespoons sliced almonds, 1 teaspoon liquid smoke, and 1 teaspoon melted butter. Cook in saucepan or bake in oven until lightly browned.

Preheat oven to 350°F. Lightly coat 13 × 9 × 2-inch baking pan with oil or spray with cooking spray. Set aside.

Combine melted butter, scallions, and 1/4 cup almonds in shallow bowl. Combine flour, sesame seed, garlic powder, salt, and pepper in shallow dish. Dip chicken breasts in butter mixture, then dredge in flour mixture. Place chicken in prepared baking pan. Bake in preheated oven 40 to 50 minutes or until chicken is no longer pink inside.

To make sauce, combine sour cream, horseradish, milk, parsley, and 2 tablespoons almonds in saucepan. Cook about 2 minutes over low heat, stirring constantly, just until heated through.

To serve, place chicken on serving plate and spoon small amount of sauce over each breast. Place remaining sauce in bowl and serve separately.

4 servings

Chicken Havana

MARINADE

- 4 tablespoons chili powder
- ½ teaspoon ground cumin
- ½ teaspoon crushed red pepper flakes (optional)
- ¼ cup lime juice (juice of about 2 limes)
- 2 tablespoons vegetable oil
- 1 tablespoon minced garlic

❖ ❖ ❖ ❖

- 8 *Gold Kist Farms* boneless, skinless, split chicken breasts

RELISH

- 2 tablespoons vegetable oil
- 2 small onions, thinly sliced, and separated into rings
- ½ small red bell pepper, cut into thin strips
- 1 can (16 ounces) black beans, drained and rinsed
- 1 can (15½ ounces) white hominy, drained and rinsed
- 1 can (15½ ounces) yellow hominy, drained and rinsed

CHILI SAUCE

- 2 cans (4 ounces each) green chilies, including liquid
- ¾ cup heavy cream
- ¾ cup dairy sour cream
- 2 tablespoons minced fresh cilantro
- Lime wedges, cilantro sprigs, and red bell pepper strips for garnish

To make marinade, place chili powder, cumin, red pepper flakes, if desired, lime juice, 2 tablespoons oil, and garlic in small bowl and stir to combine. Place chicken breasts in shallow, non-metallic dish or resealable plastic bag. Pour marinade over chicken and toss to coat. Cover or close bag and refrigerate at least 4 hours or overnight.

Preheat oven to 375° F.

To prepare relish, heat 2 tablespoons oil in large skillet. Add onion rings and pepper strips. Cook over medium heat 3 to 4 minutes or until onions are transparent. Stir in beans and white and yellow hominy. Cook 2 to 3 minutes or just until heated through. Spoon onto large ovenproof serving platter or casserole.

Remove chicken from marinade with slotted spoon and place in skillet. Discard marinade. Cook, adding additional oil if necessary, 4 to 5 minutes on each side or until chicken is no longer pink inside. Arrange chicken over relish, cover with foil, and bake in preheated oven 15 to 20 minutes.

To prepare sauce, place chilies in blender or food processor and process until smooth. Pour into medium-size saucepan and stir in cream. Bring to a gentle boil, reduce heat, and stir in sour cream and cilantro. Cook about 2 minutes or just until heated through.

Remove foil from chicken and spoon sauce over or serve sauce separately. Garnish chicken with lime wedges, cilantro, and pepper strips.

8 servings

Chicken with Apple-Pepper Sauce

INGREDIENTS

- 1/4 cup all-purpose flour
- 1 1/2 teaspoons lemon-pepper seasoning
- 1/4 teaspoon garlic powder
- 1/2 teaspoon salt or to taste
- 4 *Gold Kist Farms* boneless, skinless, split chicken breasts
- 2 tablespoons vegetable oil
- 1/2 cup apple juice
- 1/3 cup jalapeño pepper jelly
- Apple slices and parsley to garnish

Place flour in pie plate or shallow dish. Stir in lemon-pepper seasoning, garlic powder, and salt. Dredge chicken in flour mixture to coat. Shake off excess flour.

Heat oil in large skillet. Add chicken and sauté about 5 minutes on each side or until chicken is lightly browned, fork-tender, and no longer pink inside. Remove chicken from skillet, set aside, and keep warm.

Add apple juice and jelly to drippings in skillet. Cook, stirring, until jelly has melted and sauce has thickened slightly, about 4 minutes.

To serve, spoon small amount of sauce onto platter or individual serving plates and arrange chicken over sauce. Spoon remaining sauce over chicken or place in small bowl and pass at table. Garnish with apple slices and parsley.

4 servings

Chicken with Fettuccine and Vegetables

INGREDIENTS

- 2 tablespoons olive oil, divided
- 2 tablespoons butter or margarine, divided
- 1 cup chopped onion
- 4 to 5 cloves garlic, minced
- 4 cups peeled, chopped tomatoes or 1 can (28 ounces) Italian plum tomatoes, drained and chopped
- ¼ cup chopped fresh basil or 2 teaspoons dried basil
- 1 tablespoon sugar
- 2 teaspoons dried oregano
- 1 tablespoon vinegar
- Salt and freshly ground pepper to taste
- 3 to 4 *Gold Kist Farms* boneless, skinless, split chicken breasts (about 2 pounds), cut into 1-inch strips
- 2½ to 3 pounds mixed vegetables such as: asparagus, broccoli, cauliflower, carrots, mushrooms, onions, snow peas, and/or squash, cut into even, bite-size pieces (choose 2 or 3)
- 2 packages (16 ounces each) hot, cooked fettuccine or linguine
- Chopped fresh parsley to garnish (optional)
- Grated Parmesan cheese to serve

Heat 1 tablespoon oil and 1 tablespoon butter in large skillet. Add onion and cook 3 minutes. Add garlic and cook until onion is transparent. Add tomatoes, basil, sugar, oregano, vinegar, salt, and pepper. Stir to combine, cover, and simmer 15 to 20 minutes. Set aside and keep warm or cool, cover, and refrigerate overnight to allow flavors to blend. Reheat before serving.

Heat 1 tablespoon oil and 1 tablespoon butter in large skillet. Add chicken and stir-fry until thoroughly cooked and no longer pink inside, about 5 minutes. Season with salt and pepper. Remove with slotted spoon, set aside, and keep warm.

Place vegetables in steamer basket, starting with vegetables that take longest time to cook, and adding additional vegetables in appropriate order. Cover and cook over boiling water until fork-tender. Remove vegetables, set aside, and keep warm.

To serve, place pasta in large serving bowl. Spoon chicken and vegetables over pasta. Add cooked tomatoes and toss gently. Garnish with parsley, if desired, and serve with Parmesan cheese.

8 to 10 servings

Silky Spicy Chicken

INGREDIENTS

- 1½ teaspoons onion powder
- 1 teaspoon dried thyme
- ½ teaspoon black pepper
- ½ teaspoon white pepper
- ¼ teaspoon cayenne
- Salt to taste
- 2 tablespoons butter or margarine
- 1 tablespoon vegetable oil
- 2 to 3 *Gold Kist Farms* boneless, skinless, split chicken breasts (about 1½ pounds), cut into bite-size pieces
- ½ pound fresh mushrooms, thickly sliced
- 1 medium-size zucchini, julienned
- 1 medium-size tomato, peeled and chopped
- 3 small cloves garlic, minced
- 1 tablespoon cornstarch
- 1 cup milk
- 2 cups heavy cream
- 1 package (16 ounces) hot, cooked linguine
- Scallions (green onions), thinly sliced, green tops included to garnish
- Grated Parmesan cheese to serve

Place onion powder, thyme, black and white pepper, cayenne, and salt in small bowl. Stir to combine and set aside.

Melt butter with oil in large skillet. Add chicken and mushrooms. Sprinkle with reserved spice mix and stir. Cook 4 minutes. Stir in zucchini and tomato and cook 4 minutes or until vegetables are almost softened and chicken is no longer pink inside. Add garlic and cook 2 minutes. Set aside.

Place cornstarch into 4-cup measuring cup. Add small amount of milk and stir to smooth paste. Stir in remaining milk and cream slowly. Pour over reserved chicken mixture in skillet and stir. Bring to a boil, reduce heat, and simmer 5 minutes.

To serve, place hot linguine in serving dish and spoon chicken mixture over. Garnish with scallions and serve with Parmesan cheese.

6 servings

▲ Silky Spicy Chicken, facing page ▼ Chicken Lasagna Rolls with Red Pepper Sauce, page 42

Chicken Lasagna Rolls with Red Pepper Sauce

INGREDIENTS

12 lasagna noodles
3 to 4 *Gold Kist Farms* boneless, skinless, split chicken breasts (about 2 pounds)

FILLING

1 container (15 ounces) ricotta cheese
1 egg, lightly beaten
12 cooked broccoli flowerets
1 cup peeled, diced tomato
1 cup (4 ounces) shredded mozzarella cheese
¼ cup grated Parmesan cheese
1 tablespoon chopped fresh parsley
½ teaspoon dried oregano
1 teaspoon salt or to taste
Freshly ground pepper to taste

SAUCE

1 tablespoon olive oil
2 cups diced onion
2 cups diced red bell pepper
1 to 2 cloves garlic, minced
2 tablespoons butter or margarine
2 tablespoons all-purpose flour
½ cup milk
2 tablespoons chopped fresh basil
1 cup (4 ounces) shredded mozzarella cheese

❖ ❖ ❖ ❖

2 tablespoons grated Parmesan cheese

Cook noodles according to package directions. Drain and rinse in cold water. Return to pot, cover with cold water, and add 2 tablespoons vegetable oil. Set aside.

Lightly butter 12 × 9 × 2-inch casserole and set aside.

Place chicken in single layer in large saucepan and add water to cover by ½ inch. Bring to a boil, reduce heat to simmer, cover, and poach 12 to 15 minutes or until chicken is no longer pink inside. Drain, chop, and set aside.

To make filling, place ricotta cheese in bowl, stir in egg, and beat until well combined. Set aside. Place chicken, broccoli, and tomato in separate large bowl. Stir in ricotta cheese mixture, mozzarella, Parmesan cheese, parsley, oregano, salt, and pepper.

Drain noodles, pat dry, and lay flat on clean surface. Divide filling evenly on noodles and spread evenly over entire surface of each noodle. Beginning at short end, roll each noodle and place, seam-side down, in single layer in prepared casserole. Set aside.

Preheat oven to 350°F.

To make sauce, heat oil in large skillet and cook onion and bell pepper 4 minutes or until onion is transparent. Add garlic and cook 1 minute. Remove from heat and set aside. Melt butter in small saucepan. Stir in flour until blended and cook 2 minutes. Add milk slowly and cook, stirring constantly, until sauce is thickened. Add sauce to onion mixture in skillet and stir to combine. Add basil, mozzarella, salt, and pepper. Stir until cheese is melted.

Pour sauce over rolls and spread to cover. Sprinkle with Parmesan cheese. Cover with aluminum foil and bake in preheated oven 30 to 40 minutes or until hot and bubbly.

6 servings

Apple Stuffed Chicken Breasts

INGREDIENTS

- 6 *Gold Kist Farms* boneless, skinless, split chicken breasts
- 1 ½ cups diced red or green apples (about 2 apples)
- ¼ cup golden seedless raisins
- ¼ cup chopped pecans or walnuts
- 3 tablespoons minced onion
- ⅔ teaspoon dried sage
- Melted butter or margarine for brushing

GLAZE

- 4 tablespoons (½ stick) butter or margarine
- ⅓ cup apple jelly
- ¼ cup orange juice concentrate, undiluted
- ¼ cup dry sherry

Preheat oven to 350° F. Lightly grease baking pan and set aside. Place chicken breasts between sheets of plastic wrap and pound with meat mallet to ¼-inch thickness. Set aside.

Place apples, raisins, nuts, onion, and sage in bowl and stir to combine. Place 1 tablespoon apple mixture in center of each breast and roll up, enclosing filling completely. Secure with wooden toothpicks and place, seam-side down, in single layer in prepared pan. Brush with melted butter and set aside.

To make glaze, melt 4 tablespoons butter in small saucepan and stir in apple jelly, orange juice, and sherry. Simmer 3 minutes until jelly is completely melted.

Bake chicken in preheated oven, basting frequently with glaze, 30 to 45 minutes or until no longer pink inside. Remove toothpicks before serving.

6 servings

Tuscan Pesto Chicken Rolls

INGREDIENTS

4 *Gold Kist Farms* boneless, skinless, split chicken breasts
Salt and freshly ground pepper to taste
2 tablespoons pesto sauce
1 cup (4 ounces) shredded fontina cheese
4 tablespoons all-purpose flour
3 tablespoons olive oil (see Note)
1 can (14½ ounces) Italian-style stewed tomatoes, liquid reserved
1 jar (7 ounces) roasted red peppers, drained
1 tablespoon butter or margarine
½ cup diced shallots
1 clove garlic, minced
Fresh basil leaves to garnish

Note: If using non-stick skillet, decrease oil to 1 tablespoon.

Place chicken breasts between sheets of plastic wrap and pound with meat mallet to ¼-inch thickness. Season with salt and pepper, spread each with ½ tablespoon pesto sauce, and sprinkle each with ¼ cup cheese. Roll up breast halves, enclosing filling completely, and secure with wooden toothpicks. Dredge rolled breasts in flour.

Heat oil in large skillet. Add chicken rolls and cook over medium heat about 5 minutes, turning until lightly browned on all sides. Remove chicken rolls from skillet, wipe out pan, and return chicken to skillet. Cover and set aside.

Place tomatoes with liquid and roasted peppers in blender or food processor and process until smooth. Set aside. Melt butter in medium-size saucepan, add shallots and garlic and cook about 2 minutes. Add tomato mixture, salt, and pepper and simmer 5 minutes.

Press sauce through sieve over chicken rolls in skillet. Cover and cook 8 to 10 minutes or until chicken is no longer pink inside. Place rolls on serving dish and spoon sauce on top. Garnish with fresh basil leaves.

4 servings

▲ Tuscan Pesto Chicken Rolls, facing page

▼ Chicken Party Pie, page 46

Chicken Party Pie

CRUST

- 3 cups all-purpose flour
- ½ teaspoon salt
- ½ pound (2 sticks) butter, cut into chunks (no substitution)
- 1 egg yolk
- 3 tablespoons ice water

FILLING

- 6 tablespoons (¾ stick) butter or margarine, divided
- 2 *Gold Kist Farms* boneless, skinless, split chicken breasts (about 1 pound), cut into bite-size pieces or ½-inch strips
- 1 pound fresh mushrooms, sliced
- 3 scallions (green onions) sliced, green tops included
- 1 red bell pepper, chopped
- 3 cloves garlic, minced
- 1 package (10 ounces) frozen tiny peas
- 3 tablespoons all-purpose flour
- 1 cup milk
- ½ teaspoon dried tarragon
- ⅛ teaspoon nutmeg
- Salt and freshly ground pepper to taste
- 1 cup (4 ounces) Havarti cheese, cut into small pieces

❖ ❖ ❖ ❖

- 1 egg, lightly beaten

To make crust, place flour in large bowl and stir in salt. Cut in butter with pastry blender or 2 knives until mixture resembles coarse crumbs. Place egg yolk in small bowl or cup measure. Add ice water and stir until well combined. Sprinkle over flour mixture, 1 tablespoon at a time, and toss with fork until dough binds together. Gather in hands and form into ball. Divide dough into 2 smooth balls and wrap separately in plastic wrap. Place in refrigerator to chill while preparing filling or overnight.

To make filling, melt 3 tablespoons butter in large skillet. Add chicken and cook until no longer pink inside, about 5 minutes. Add mushrooms, scallions, and bell pepper. Cook 5 minutes or until vegetables are almost tender. Add garlic and cook 2 to 3 minutes. Spoon into large bowl, stir in frozen peas, and set aside.

Melt remaining 3 tablespoons butter in same skillet. Stir in flour and cook, stirring, 2 minutes. Add milk slowly, stirring constantly, until smooth and slightly thickened. Add tarragon, nutmeg, salt, and pepper. Stir to blend. Add cheese and stir until melted. Pour sauce over chicken mixture and stir gently. Set aside.

Preheat oven to 425°F.

Remove 1 ball of dough from refrigerator, unwrap, and place on lightly floured surface. Flour rolling pin and roll out dough to 12-inch circle. Fold dough over rolling pin and ease into 10-inch deep-dish pie plate. Do not trim edges. Spoon filling into pie plate. Roll out remaining dough to 12-inch circle. Unfold over filling and trim edges to 1 inch beyond rim of pie plate. Fold edges under, press together, and flute. Cut slits in center of top crust to vent. Place egg in small dish, beat with 1 tablespoon water and brush over top crust. Bake in preheated oven about 30 minutes or until crust is golden.

4 to 6 servings

Mediterranean Rim Chicken

INGREDIENTS

- 1 jar (8 ounces) sun-dried tomatoes marinated in oil, drained and chopped, liquid reserved
- 3 to 4 *Gold Kist Farms* boneless, skinless, split chicken breasts (about 2 pounds), cut into bite-size pieces
- 1 cup chopped onion
- 2 cloves garlic, minced
- ½ pound fresh mushrooms, sliced
- ¼ cup Marsala
- 1 can (7 ounces) artichoke bottoms, drained and quartered
- 2 cups dairy sour cream
- Salt and freshly ground pepper to taste

CRUST

- ½ cup fresh sourdough or plain bread crumbs
- 1 cup grated Parmesan cheese
- 3 cups cooked rice, cooled
- 1 cup (4 ounces) shredded Swiss or Gruyére cheese

Preheat oven to 400° F. Generously butter bottom and sides of 2-quart casserole and set aside.

Heat liquid reserved from tomatoes in large skillet over medium-high heat. Add chicken and cook 2 to 3 minutes or until outside is no longer pink. Add onion, garlic, and mushrooms and cook until vegetables are softened. Stir in Marsala and cook until most of liquid has been absorbed. Stir in sun-dried tomatoes and artichoke bottoms. Remove from heat and stir in sour cream, salt, and pepper. Set aside.

Combine bread crumbs and Parmesan cheese in small bowl. Sprinkle half of mixture on bottom and sides of prepared casserole.

Place rice and Swiss cheese in large bowl and stir to combine. Press half of mixture onto bottom of dish over crumb mixture. Spoon chicken filling over and top with remaining rice mixture, spreading to edge of dish. Top with remaining bread crumb mixture and bake, uncovered, in preheated oven 30 minutes or until top is golden.

6 to 8 servings

Guadalajara Chicken Olé

INGREDIENTS

- 5 to 6 *Gold Kist Farms* boneless, skinless, split chicken breasts (about 3 pounds)
- 4 tablespoons (½ stick) butter or margarine
- 1½ cups chopped onion
- 1 medium-size green bell pepper, chopped
- ¼ cup all-purpose flour
- 2 cups milk
- 1½ cups chicken broth
- 1 cup dairy sour cream
- 2 cans (4 ounces each) green chilies, drained and chopped
- 2 cans (2¼ ounces each) pitted black olives, drained and sliced
- ¼ cup seeded and chopped jalapeño peppers
- 2 teaspoons seasoned salt
- 2 teaspoons ground cumin
- 8 small corn or flour tortillas, torn into bite-size pieces
- 4 cups (1 pound) shredded sharp Cheddar cheese
- 2 cups (8 ounces) shredded Monterey Jack cheese

Preheat oven to 375°F. Grease 3-quart casserole and set aside.

Place chicken in single layer in large saucepan and add enough water to cover by ½ inch. Bring to a boil, reduce heat to simmer, cover, and poach 12 to 15 minutes or until chicken is no longer pink inside. Drain and set aside to cool.

Melt butter in large saucepan. Add onion and green pepper and cook until onion is transparent. Stir in flour and cook, stirring, 2 minutes. Reduce heat and add milk and chicken broth slowly, stirring constantly. Cook, stirring, until sauce is thickened. Stir in sour cream, chilies, olives, jalapeño peppers, seasoned salt, and cumin.

Cut chicken into bite-size pieces and arrange layer of chicken in bottom of prepared casserole. Cover with layer of tortillas, sauce, and cheeses. Repeat layers in same order until all ingredients have been used, making as many layers as possible. Bake in preheated oven 30 minutes or until casserole is heated through and cheese is melted and lightly browned.

6 to 8 servings

Note: Casserole may be frozen prior to baking. Thaw in refrigerator and bake 45 minutes to 1 hour.

▲ Guadalajara Chicken Olé, facing page

▼ Ricotta Chicken Pie, page 50

Ricotta Chicken Pie

CRUST

- ½ cup ricotta cheese
- 5 tablespoons butter or margarine, softened
- 1 cup sifted all-purpose flour
- ½ teaspoon salt

FILLING

- ½ pound bulk pork sausage
- 3 to 4 *Gold Kist Farms* boneless, skinless, split chicken breasts (about 2 pounds), cut into bite-size pieces
- ¼ cup chopped onion
- 1 cup ricotta cheese
- ¾ cup milk
- 4 eggs
- Salt and freshly ground pepper to taste
- ¾ cup (3 ounces) shredded Swiss cheese
- 2 tablespoons freshly chopped parsley

To make crust, place ½ cup ricotta cheese and butter in mixer bowl or food processor and beat or process until smooth. Blend in flour and salt. Form dough into ball, wrap in plastic wrap, and place in refrigerator to chill about 30 minutes.

Preheat oven to 450°F.

Roll out dough on lightly floured surface to 12-inch circle. Place in deep 9-inch pie plate, pressing gently to fit. Trim edge with sharp knife or scissors to 1 inch beyond rim of pie plate. Fold edge under and flute edge. Prick holes in bottom with fork. Cover and chill 10 to 15 minutes. Bake in preheated oven 5 minutes. Cool on rack. Reduce oven temperature to 375°F.

To make filling, place sausage in large skillet over medium-high heat and cook 3 to 4 minutes, stirring. Add chicken and onion and cook, stirring, until sausage is browned and chicken is no longer pink inside. Drain excess fat and set mixture aside. Beat 1 cup ricotta cheese, milk, eggs, salt, and pepper in medium-size bowl. Stir in reserved chicken-sausage mixture, Swiss cheese, and parsley.

Pour filling into prebaked crust. Bake 40 to 50 minutes in preheated oven or until filling is set. Let stand 5 minutes before serving.

6 servings

Chicken Casserole Southwestern-Style

INGREDIENTS

4 tablespoons olive oil, divided
4 *Gold Kist Farms* boneless, skinless, split chicken breasts
1 medium-size onion, chopped
1 can (4 ounces) green chilies, drained and chopped
3 cloves garlic, minced
1 can (14 ounces) plum tomatoes, drained and chopped
1 tablespoon red wine vinegar
4 teaspoons ground cumin
½ teaspoon dried oregano
Salt and freshly ground pepper to taste
1 can (15 ounces) black beans, drained and rinsed
1 cup (4 ounces) shredded Monterey Jack cheese
1 cup (4 ounces) shredded Cheddar cheese

Preheat oven to 350°F.

Heat 2 tablespoons oil in large skillet. Add chicken and sauté 2 minutes on each side. Remove from skillet and place in single layer in medium-size casserole. Set aside.

Add 2 tablespoons oil to skillet and cook onion and green chilies 4 minutes or until onion is transparent. Add garlic and cook 2 minutes. Stir in tomatoes, vinegar, cumin, oregano, salt, and pepper. Cover and simmer 5 minutes. Add beans and cook 5 minutes.

Spoon bean mixture over chicken in casserole and sprinkle with cheeses. Cover dish with aluminum foil and bake in preheated oven 20 to 30 minutes or until heated through and cheese is melted.

4 servings

Variation: Cut chicken breasts into bite-size pieces and stir-fry in 2 tablespoons oil until no longer pink inside. Place in casserole and proceed as above.

Chicken-Corn Bread Casserole

INGREDIENTS

- 4 tablespoons (½ stick) butter or margarine
- 3 to 4 *Gold Kist Farms* boneless, skinless, split chicken breasts (about 2 pounds), cut into bite-size pieces
- 1 cup chopped onion
- 1 cup dairy sour cream
- 1 can (4 ounces) mushroom pieces, drained
- ½ cup (2 ounces) shredded Cheddar cheese
- ½ teaspoon dried thyme
- ¼ teaspoon dried sage
- Salt to taste

CORN BREAD

- 1 cup yellow cornmeal
- ½ cup all-purpose flour
- 1½ teaspoons baking powder
- 1 teaspoon salt
- ⅛ teaspoon cayenne
- 1 can (17 ounces) creamed corn
- ⅓ cup milk
- 1 egg, lightly beaten
- ½ cup (2 ounces) shredded Cheddar cheese

Preheat oven to 425° F. Grease 9-inch square baking pan and set aside.

Melt butter in large skillet and cook chicken and onion until chicken is no longer pink inside and onion is transparent. Stir in sour cream, mushrooms, ½ cup Cheddar cheese, thyme, sage, and salt. Remove from heat and set aside.

Place cornmeal, flour, baking powder, 1 teaspoon salt, and cayenne in large bowl and stir to combine. Place corn, milk, and egg in separate bowl and beat until well mixed. Stir into dry ingredients until well blended and pour into prepared dish. Top with chicken mixture and bake in preheated oven 15 minutes. Sprinkle ½ cup Cheddar cheese on top and bake 25 minutes or until top is lightly browned. Let stand 10 minutes and cut into squares.

4 to 6 servings

Variation: About 6 ounces fresh mushrooms, sliced, may be substituted for canned mushrooms. Add to skillet and cook with chicken and onion.

Savory Chicken Stew

INGREDIENTS

- 2 to 3 tablespoons vegetable oil
- 1½ to 2 pounds *Gold Kist Farms* boneless, skinless, split chicken breasts (2 to 3) or thighs (6 to 8), cut into 2-inch pieces
- 1 large red onion, chopped
- 1 cup chopped green bell pepper
- 6 to 8 cloves garlic, crushed
- 1½ teaspoons curry powder or to taste
- 2 cans (28 ounces each) whole peeled tomatoes, chopped and liquid reserved
- 1½ tablespoons browning sauce
- ¼ teaspoon mace
- 3 tablespoons chopped fresh parsley
- ⅓ cup raisins or currants
- Salt and freshly ground pepper to taste
- Hot, cooked rice to serve
- ½ cup slivered almonds to garnish

Heat oil in large skillet, add chicken, and cook until lightly browned. Remove to dish with slotted spoon and set aside.

Add onion, bell pepper, garlic, and curry to drippings in skillet. Cook over low heat about 4 minutes or until onion is transparent. Return chicken to pan. Add chopped tomatoes and liquid, browning sauce, mace, parsley, raisins, salt, and pepper. Cover and simmer 30 minutes or until chicken is no longer pink inside, stirring occasionally.

To serve, spoon rice into soup bowls and spoon chicken stew over rice. Sprinkle with almonds and serve immediately.

8 to 10 servings

Hsi Chang Chicken Stir-Fry

SAUCE

4 teaspoons cornstarch
¼ cup dry sherry or saké
¼ cup soy sauce
2 tablespoons light corn syrup
1 tablespoon vinegar
¼ teaspoon ground ginger

❖ ❖ ❖ ❖

2 *Gold Kist Farms* boneless, skinless, split chicken breasts (about 1 pound), cut into bite-size pieces
Salt and freshly ground pepper to taste
¼ cup vegetable oil
1 medium-size green or red bell pepper, cut into strips
1½ cups thickly sliced fresh mushrooms
6 scallions (green onions), cut into 2-inch pieces, green tops included
1 can (8 ounces) sliced water chestnuts, drained
1 can (8 ounces) pineapple chunks, drained
2 pimientos, drained and sliced (optional)
1 package (6 ounces) frozen snow peas, thawed (optional)
Hot, cooked rice to serve

To make sauce, place cornstarch in small bowl and stir in ¼ cup water to make smooth paste. Add sherry, soy sauce, corn syrup, vinegar, and ginger. Stir to blend and set aside.

Season chicken with salt and pepper. Heat wok or large skillet over high heat and add oil by pouring around sides of wok. When oil is hot, add chicken and stir-fry 6 to 8 minutes or until no longer pink inside. Remove chicken to dish with slotted spoon and add bell pepper to wok. Stir-fry until tender but still crisp, about 2 minutes. Remove with slotted spoon.

Add mushrooms and scallions to wok and stir-fry until softened. Return chicken and bell pepper to wok and add water chestnuts, pineapple, pimientos, and snow peas, if desired. Add sauce, stir, and cook about 3 minutes or until vegetables are heated through and sauce has thickened.

Serve immediately over rice.

4 servings

Versatile Chicken Stir-Fry

SAUCE

2 tablespoons soy sauce
2 tablespoons white vinegar
1 teaspoon sesame oil
1 teaspoon sugar
1 scallion (green onion), thinly sliced, green top included
1 clove garlic, minced
1 teaspoon chili sauce (optional)

❖ ❖ ❖ ❖

3 to 4 tablespoons peanut or vegetable oil
2 *Gold Kist Farms* boneless, skinless, split chicken breasts (about 1 pound), cut into strips

Choice of 2 or 3 of any of the following vegetables:

12 small broccoli flowerets
½ pound asparagus spears, cut into 1-inch lengths
¼ pound fresh mushrooms, sliced
¼ pound fresh bean sprouts
1 package (10 ounces) frozen sugar snap peas, thawed
1 medium-size red or green bell pepper, thinly sliced
1 medium-size onion, thinly sliced

❖ ❖ ❖ ❖

Hot, cooked rice to serve

Note: Sauce and ingredients may be doubled.

To make sauce, place soy sauce, vinegar, sesame oil, ¼ cup hot water, sugar, scallion, garlic, and chili sauce in small bowl. Beat with whisk until well combined. Set aside.

Heat oil in wok or large skillet. Add chicken and stir-fry 5 minutes or until chicken is no longer pink inside. Remove chicken with slotted spoon and set aside.

Add vegetables to wok beginning with vegetables that take longest time to cook. Depending on choice of vegetables, stir-fry about 3 to 6 minutes or until vegetables are tender but still crisp. Add sauce and reserved chicken. Stir to coat and stir-fry 2 to 3 minutes or until heated.

Serve over rice.

4 to 6 servings

Chicken Thighs with Black Bean Relish

INGREDIENTS

6 to 8 *Gold Kist Farms* boneless, skinless chicken thighs (about 1½ pounds)
2 tablespoons olive oil
1 clove garlic, minced
Salt and freshly ground pepper to taste

RELISH

1 can (16 ounces) black beans, drained and rinsed
⅔ cup thinly sliced scallions (green onions), green tops included
1 medium-size tomato, peeled and diced
½ cup chopped red bell pepper
1 clove garlic, minced
2 tablespoons cider vinegar
1 teaspoon sugar
½ to 1 teaspoon ground cumin

❖ ❖ ❖ ❖

1 cup (4 ounces) shredded Monterey Jack cheese
Hot, cooked yellow rice to serve (see Note)

Note: Yellow rice can be found in rice section or ethnic food section of supermarket.

Place chicken thighs between sheets of plastic wrap and pound with meat mallet to ¼-inch thickness. Heat oil in large skillet and brown chicken on all sides, about 12 minutes. Add 1 clove garlic and cook 2 to 3 minutes or until chicken is fork-tender and opaque. Season chicken with salt and pepper and place in single layer in casserole. Set aside and keep warm.

Preheat oven to 400°F.

To make relish, place beans, scallions, tomato, bell pepper, 1 clove garlic, vinegar, sugar, cumin, salt, and pepper in bowl and stir to combine. Spoon over chicken thighs and sprinkle with cheese. Bake in preheated oven 10 to 15 minutes or until heated through. Serve with yellow rice.

6 to 8 servings

Variation: Substitute 2 to 3 boneless, skinless, split chicken breasts for boneless, skinless chicken thighs and proceed as above.

Chicken Thighs
with Black Bean Relish,
facing page

Chicken Thighs Wellington

INGREDIENTS

1 package (17¼ ounces) puff pastry sheets
8 *Gold Kist Farms* boneless, skinless chicken thighs (about 4 ounces each)
Salt and freshly ground pepper to taste
4 tablespoons (½ stick) butter
1 pound fresh mushrooms, minced
6 to 8 scallions (green onions), thinly sliced, green tops included
2 tablespoons all-purpose flour
¼ teaspoon dried thyme
½ cup chopped cooked ham

Variation: Substitute 2 phyllo leaves per chicken roll for puff pastry.

Remove pastry from package and place on plate to thaw about 20 minutes.

Place chicken thighs between sheets of plastic wrap and pound with meat mallet to ¼-inch thickness. Season with salt and pepper and set aside.

Melt butter in large skillet over medium-high heat. Add mushrooms and scallions and cook until tender, about 5 minutes. Add flour, thyme, salt, and pepper. Cook, stirring, about 2 minutes until slightly thickened. Stir in ham and remove from heat. Place 1 tablespoon ham mixture on each thigh and roll up, enclosing filling completely. Set aside.

Preheat oven to 350°F.

Sprinkle work surface lightly with flour. Gently unfold 1 sheet of pastry and lay flat on work surface. Lightly flour rolling pin and roll out pastry to 14-inch square. Cut into four 7-inch squares and spread about 1 tablespoon ham mixture on each square, leaving ½-inch border. Place 1 chicken roll on each square. Moisten edges of pastry, fold up over chicken, and press to seal. Place, seam-side down, on ungreased baking sheet. Repeat with second sheet of pastry and remaining ingredients.

Bake in preheated oven 30 to 35 minutes or until pastry is golden brown.

8 filled squares

Chicken Dijon

INGREDIENTS

- 8 to 12 *Gold Kist Farms* chicken drumsticks (about 2 to 3 pounds)
- Salt and freshly ground pepper to taste
- 2 tablespoons firmly packed brown sugar
- 1/3 cup Dijon-style mustard
- 1/4 cup vegetable oil
- 1 cup finely ground dry bread crumbs

SAUCE

- 1/2 cup creamy-style cottage cheese
- 1/2 cup dairy sour cream or yogurt
- 1 tablespoon Dijon-style mustard
- 1/4 cup thinly sliced scallions (green onions), green tops included
- Salt and freshly ground pepper to taste

Preheat oven to 375° F. Lightly grease baking pan and set aside.

Season drumsticks with salt and pepper. Place brown sugar, 1/3 cup mustard, and oil in small bowl and stir to combine. Brush drumsticks with mixture, coating completely.

Place bread crumbs on plate and roll coated drumsticks in crumbs to cover on all sides. Place in prepared pan and bake in preheated oven 45 minutes or until juices run clear when thickest part of drumstick is pierced with fork.

To make sauce, place cottage cheese, sour cream, and 1 tablespoon mustard in food processor or blender. Process until well blended. Spoon into small serving bowl and stir in scallions, salt, and pepper. Use immediately or cover and refrigerate until ready to use.

To serve, place drumsticks on serving plate and pass bowl of sauce separately.

4 to 6 servings

Variation: For appetizers, substitute 24 to 36 drummettes (2 to 3 pounds) for drumsticks or about 20 whole wings (about 4 pounds), cut into wingettes. Prepare as above and bake in preheated oven 25 to 30 minutes. To serve, arrange on platter with bowl of dipping sauce in center of platter.

Oven Chicken Fricassee

INGREDIENTS

- 1 cup all-purpose flour
- ½ teaspoon dried thyme
- Salt and freshly ground pepper to taste
- 3 to 3½ pound *Gold Kist Farms* whole chicken, cut up, or chicken parts of choice
- 3 to 4 tablespoons vegetable or olive oil
- 1 jar (16 ounces) boiled whole onions, drained
- ½ pound fresh mushrooms, cut in half
- 1 cup chicken broth
- ¾ cup dry white wine
- 2 egg yolks
- ½ cup heavy cream
- 1 tablespoon chopped fresh parsley to garnish
- 6 slices bacon, cooked and crumbled to garnish (optional)
- Hot, cooked rice or noodles to serve (optional)

Preheat oven to 350° F.

Place flour in pie plate. Stir in thyme, salt, and pepper. Dredge chicken pieces in flour mixture to coat on all sides. Heat oil in large skillet. Add chicken to skillet and cook over medium-high heat 10 to 15 minutes or until chicken is browned on all sides. Remove chicken pieces with tongs and place in single layer in 13 × 9 × 2-inch baking pan. Set aside.

Add onions and mushrooms to skillet and cook, stirring, about 5 minutes or until onions are lightly browned and mushrooms are softened. Spoon over chicken. Pour broth and wine over chicken and bake in preheated oven 45 minutes or until chicken is tender and juices run clear when thighs are pierced with fork.

Remove chicken, onions, and mushrooms to serving platter with slotted spoon, set aside, and keep warm.

To make sauce, pour liquid from baking pan into medium-size saucepan. Place egg yolks and cream in 2-cup measuring cup and beat to combine. Off heat, add to liquid in saucepan very slowly, beating constantly. Cook over low heat, stirring constantly, until sauce is thickened. Season with salt and pepper and pour over chicken and vegetables. Garnish with parsley and bacon, if desired.

Serve with rice or noodles.

4 to 6 servings

Chicken Wailua

INGREDIENTS

- 3 to 3 1/2 pound *Gold Kist Farms* whole chicken, quartered
- Salt and freshly ground pepper to taste
- 4 tablespoons (1/2 stick) butter, melted, divided
- 1/2 cup chicken broth
- 1 can (8 ounces) pineapple slices, juice reserved
- 1/4 cup firmly packed brown sugar
- 1/4 teaspoon ground ginger
- 2 teaspoons soy sauce
- 2 teaspoons cornstarch
- 2 maraschino cherries, cut in half
- Hot, cooked rice to serve (optional)

Preheat oven to 350°F.

Season chicken quarters with salt and pepper, brush with melted butter to coat, and place in 13 × 9 × 2-inch baking dish. Pour broth around chicken and bake in preheated oven 30 minutes, basting occasionally with remaining melted butter.

To make sauce, pour pineapple juice into measuring cup and add water, if necessary, to make 1/2 cup. Pour into saucepan and add sugar, ginger, and soy sauce. Place cornstarch in small dish. Stir in just enough water to make smooth paste. Stir into saucepan and cook over medium heat, stirring until syrupy.

Remove baking pan from oven. Place 1 pineapple slice on top of each chicken quarter, and place half cherry in center of pineapple slice.

Spoon sauce over and bake 15 minutes, basting occasionally, until chicken is tender and juices run clear when thighs are pierced with fork. Remove to serving dish and serve with rice.

4 servings

Oven Barbecue Chicken

INGREDIENTS

3 to $3\frac{1}{2}$ pound *Gold Kist Farms* whole chicken, cut up, or chicken parts of choice

MARINADE/SAUCE

- ¼ cup red wine vinegar
- 2 tablespoons Worcestershire sauce
- ¾ cup firmly packed light brown sugar
- ¾ cup ketchup
- 1¼ tablespoons dry mustard
- 1 teaspoon paprika
- ⅛ teaspoon hot pepper sauce
- 1 teaspoon salt or to taste
- ½ teaspoon freshly ground pepper or to taste
- 1 small onion, thinly sliced

Place chicken in large saucepan and add enough water to cover by 1 inch. Cover and simmer 15 minutes. Remove chicken with tongs and place in non-metallic baking pan. Set aside.

Place remaining ingredients, except onion, in blender or food processor and process until thoroughly blended. Stir in onion and pour over chicken pieces. Cover and refrigerate at least 1 hour or overnight.

Preheat oven to 350° F.

Place covered pan with chicken and marinade in preheated oven. Bake 1 hour or until chicken is tender and juices run clear when thighs are pierced with fork.

To serve, remove chicken from baking pan with tongs and arrange on serving platter. Pour sauce into gravy boat or bowl and pass separately.

4 to 6 servings

Roast Chicken with Sausage-Apple Stuffing

INGREDIENTS

3½ to 4 pound *Gold Kist Farms* whole chicken

STUFFING

- 1 tablespoon butter or margarine
- 1 cup thinly sliced scallions (green onions), green tops included
- 1 pound hot or mild bulk pork sausage
- 1 egg, beaten
- 2 cups cubed French bread
- 1 medium-size apple, unpeeled, cored, and chopped
- Salt and freshly ground pepper to taste

HERB BUTTER

- ½ cup (1 stick) butter or margarine
- ½ teaspoon dried sage
- ½ teaspoon dried thyme
- ½ teaspoon dried rosemary
- Salt and freshly ground pepper to taste

Note: Stuffing, all of it, or excess that does not fit in cavity of chicken, can be baked in covered casserole. Bake about 30 minutes. Uncover during last 5 minutes of cooking if crisp top is desired. If chicken is roasted unstuffed, reduce cooking time 10 to 15 minutes. To add color to surface of chicken, sprinkle with paprika before roasting.

Remove giblets and reserve for use another time. Rinse chicken inside and out, pat dry, and set aside.

To make stuffing, melt 1 tablespoon butter in skillet and cook scallions just until softened. Remove with slotted spoon and place in large bowl. Add sausage to skillet, stir to crumble, and cook until sausage is browned. Drain fat and spoon sausage mixture into bowl with scallions. Add egg, bread cubes, apple, salt, and pepper. Mix with large fork until well combined. Spoon loosely into chicken cavity. Truss cavity to close, fold wing tips back under upper part of wings, and tie legs together.

Preheat oven to 350°F.

To make herb butter, melt ½ cup butter in small saucepan. Stir in sage, thyme, rosemary, salt, and pepper. Brush over surface of chicken, reserving unused herb butter for basting.

Place chicken, breast-side up, on rack in roasting pan. Roast in preheated oven 20 minutes per pound or until juices run clear when thighs are pierced with fork, temperature on meat thermometer is 180°F, and center of stuffing is 165°F. Baste chicken with reserved herb butter and pan drippings every 10 to 15 minutes.

Remove chicken to carving board, untie legs, and remove trussing. Spoon stuffing into serving dish and keep warm until ready to serve. Let chicken stand 10 to 15 minutes before carving. Use pan drippings to make gravy, if desired.

4 to 6 servings

Cornish Hens Roma

INGREDIENTS

4 *Gold Kist Farms* Cornish Hens (1 pound 6 ounces each)
Salt and freshly ground pepper to taste
1 teaspoon dried oregano
Melted butter or margarine for basting

SAUCE

¼ cup olive oil
1 onion, chopped
3 small bell peppers (1 red, 1 green and 1 yellow), cut into thin strips
2 cloves garlic, minced
1 can (28 ounces) tomatoes
1 teaspoon sugar

❖ ❖ ❖ ❖

1 package (16 ounces) hot, cooked spaghetti
¼ cup shredded fresh basil to garnish (optional)
½ cup sliced pitted black olives to garnish
Grated Parmesan cheese to serve

Preheat oven to 400°F.

Remove giblets and set aside for use another time. Rinse hens and pat dry. Rub surface with salt, pepper, and oregano. Tie legs together and place hens, breast-side up, on rack in roasting pan.

Brush with melted butter. Reduce oven temperature to 350°F. Roast in preheated oven 1 hour to 1 hour 15 minutes, basting frequently, until temperature on meat thermometer is 180°F and juices run clear when thighs are pierced with fork.

To prepare sauce, heat oil in large skillet. Add onion and pepper and cook about 3 minutes. Add garlic and cook until onion is transparent. Stir in tomatoes with their liquid, sugar, salt, and pepper. Simmer 4 to 5 minutes or until thickened.

To serve, place spaghetti on large platter. Arrange hens on spaghetti and spoon sauce over. Sprinkle with basil and garnish with black olives. Place cheese in small bowl and pass at table.

4 to 6 servings

Cornish Hens Roma,
facing page

Dutch Oven Cornish Hens

INGREDIENTS

4 *Gold Kist Farms* Cornish hens (1 pound 6 ounces each)
Salt and freshly ground pepper to taste
1 medium-size onion, quartered
1 medium-size green apple, cored and quartered
2 tablespoons olive oil
1 teaspoon paprika
5 to 6 medium-size potatoes, peeled and cut in half
6 to 8 carrots, cut into chunks
3 stalks celery, cut into 1-inch pieces
3 cloves garlic
2 to 3 bay leaves
1 cup dry white wine

Preheat oven to 400° F. Grease Dutch oven or large baking pan and set aside.

Remove giblets and set aside for use another time. Rinse hens, pat dry, and season inside and out with salt and pepper. Tuck wing tips back under upper part of wings. Place onion quarter and apple quarter inside each hen cavity. Tie legs together. Rub hens all over with oil and sprinkle with paprika. Place hens in single layer, breast-side up, in prepared pan.

Arrange potatoes, carrots, celery, garlic, and bay leaves around hens in pan. Pour in wine. Cover with pan cover or aluminum foil and bake in preheated oven 50 minutes. Remove cover and baste hens with pan drippings. Bake, uncovered, 15 to 20 minutes to brown hens. Turn with tongs after 8 minutes to brown entire surface. Bake until temperature on meat thermometer is 180° F and juices run clear when thighs are pierced with fork.

To serve, remove and discard bay leaves and apple and onion quarters in cavities. Place hens on serving platter and surround with vegetables.

6 to 8 servings

Caribbean-Style Cornish Hens

INGREDIENTS

- 4 *Gold Kist Farms* Cornish Hens (1 pound 6 ounces each)
- Salt and freshly ground pepper to taste
- 1 cup Madeira, divided
- ½ cup orange juice concentrate, undiluted
- 1 cup unpeeled, cored, and chopped apple
- 1 cup chopped celery
- 1 cup chopped onion
- 1 medium-size orange, unpeeled, seeds removed, and chopped (see Note)
- 1 cup seedless green and/or red grapes
- ½ cup raisins

Note: Use blender or food processor to chop orange or dice by hand.

Remove giblets and reserve for use another time. Split hens lengthwise, rinse, pat dry, and season both sides with salt and pepper. Place in large non-metallic dish or resealable plastic bag.

Combine ½ cup Madeira with orange juice and pour over hens. Cover or close bag and place in refrigerator at least 2 hours or overnight, if possible.

To make stuffing, place apple, celery, onion, orange, grapes, raisins, and remaining ½ cup Madeira in bowl and mix well. Cover and refrigerate at least 2 hours or overnight, if possible.

Preheat oven to 350° F.

Place rack in large roasting pan. Remove hens from marinade and discard marinade. (Do not use to baste hens.) Place hens, skin-side down, on rack. Set half of stuffing aside. Spoon remaining half over hens, dividing evenly and filling cavities.

Roast, uncovered, in preheated oven 30 to 40 minutes, basting frequently, until temperature on meat thermometer is 170° F and juices run clear when thighs are pierced with fork.

When cooked, spoon remaining stuffing over cooked stuffing and cook 5 minutes or until stuffing is warmed through.

6 to 8 servings

Sopa de Pollo y Frijoles, page 78

Light Meals

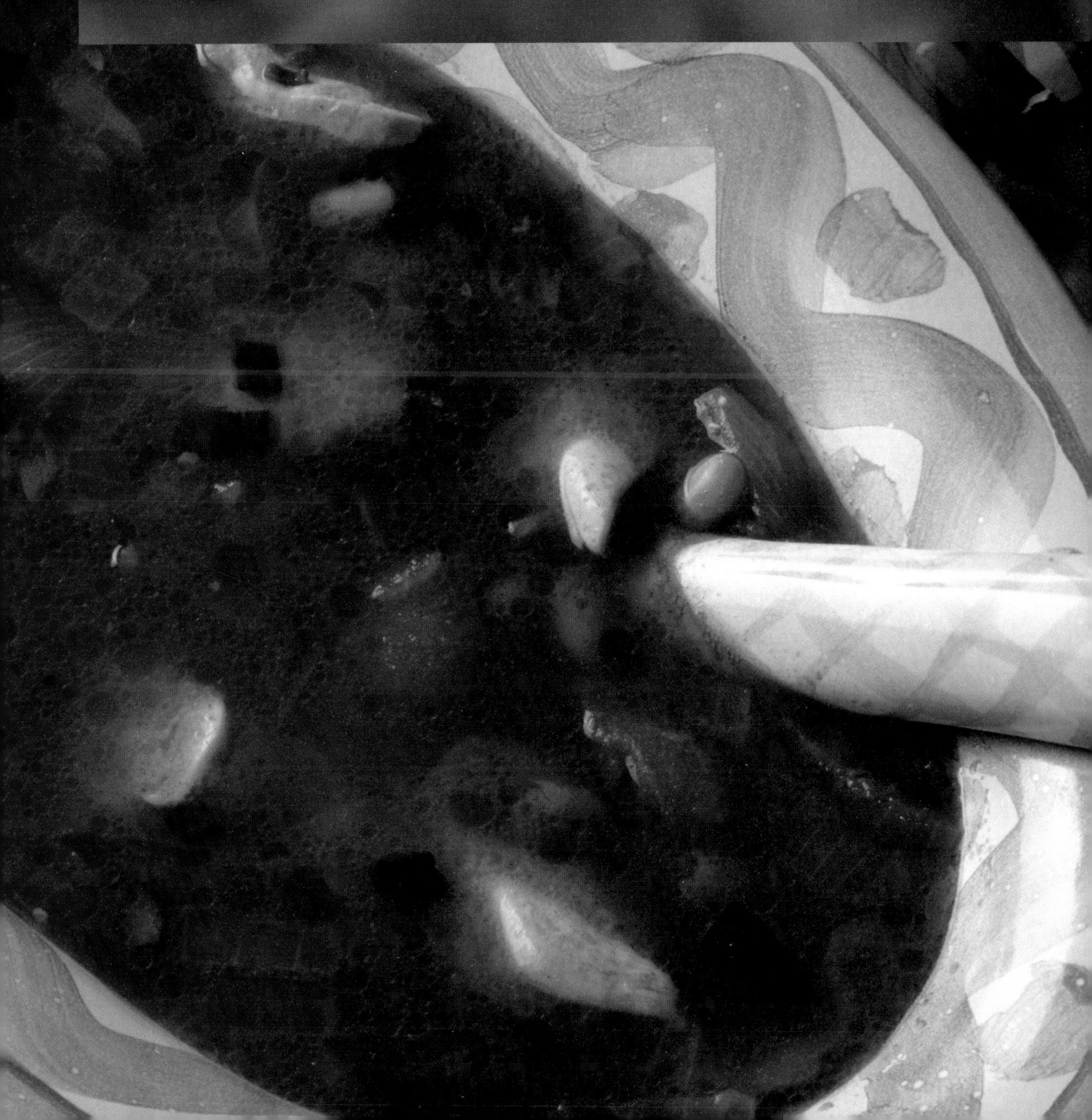

Chicken Salad with Cajun Dressing

INGREDIENTS

- 2 *Gold Kist Farms* boneless, skinless, split chicken breasts (about 1 pound)
- 1 can (15 ounces) black beans, drained and rinsed
- 1 cup cooked rice
- 1 can (11 ounces) whole-kernel corn, drained
- 1 avocado, pitted, peeled, and cut into chunks
- 12 cherry tomatoes, cut in half

DRESSING

- 3/4 cup olive oil
- 1/4 cup balsamic vinegar
- 1/2 cup ketchup
- 2 cloves garlic, crushed
- 1 tablespoon brown mustard
- 1/2 teaspoon cayenne
- 2 tablespoons minced fresh parsley

❖ ❖ ❖ ❖

Spinach or lettuce leaves to serve

Place chicken in single layer in saucepan. Add enough water to cover by 1/2 inch. Bring to a boil, reduce heat, cover, and poach 12 to 15 minutes or until chicken is no longer pink inside. Drain and set aside to cool. Cut into bite-size pieces, place in bowl, cover, and place in refrigerator to chill.

Place chicken, beans, rice, corn, avocado, and cherry tomatoes in large bowl. Toss gently and set aside.

To make dressing, place olive oil, vinegar, ketchup, garlic, mustard, cayenne, and parsley in 2-cup measuring cup. Beat with whisk until well combined. Pour desired amount of dressing over salad and toss gently to coat. Place remaining dressing in small pitcher and pass at table.

To serve, line salad bowl or individual serving plates with spinach leaves and spoon salad into center of bowl or onto plates.

4 main course servings or 6 to 8 side dish servings

Hearts of Palm-Chicken Salad

INGREDIENTS

6 *Gold Kist Farms* boneless, skinless, split chicken breasts (about 3 pounds)
1 cup dry white wine
½ cup chicken broth or water
2 cloves garlic, minced
¼ teaspoon dried tarragon
¼ teaspoon dried basil
1 can (14 ounces) hearts of palm, drained and cut into bite-size pieces, divided
6 cups torn mixed salad greens
1 red onion, cut into thin rings
1 tomato, seeded and chopped

DRESSING

⅓ cup olive oil
¼ cup balsamic vinegar
2 tablespoons Dijon-style mustard
1 clove garlic, minced
½ teaspoon crushed red pepper flakes
¼ teaspoon dried tarragon
¼ teaspoon dried thyme
¼ teaspoon dried basil
Salt to taste

❖ ❖ ❖ ❖

1 tomato, cut into wedges to garnish

Place chicken in single layer in large skillet. Add wine and enough chicken broth to cover chicken by ½ inch. Add 2 cloves garlic, tarragon, and basil. Bring to a boil, reduce heat, cover, and poach 12 to 15 minutes or until chicken is no longer pink inside. Set aside to cool in liquid about 15 minutes. Remove from liquid and cut into 1-inch strips. Place in bowl, cover, and refrigerate until ready to serve.

When ready to serve, set aside about 1 cup hearts of palm for garnish. Chop remaining hearts of palm and combine with chicken. Add salad greens, onion, and chopped tomato. Toss gently and set aside.

To make dressing, place olive oil, vinegar, and mustard in 2-cup measuring cup or screw-top jar. Beat with whisk to combine or shake vigorously. Add 1 clove garlic, pepper flakes, herbs, and salt. Beat or shake again until well combined. Refrigerate at least 15 minutes to blend flavors.

Toss dressing with salad and spoon into salad bowl or onto individual serving plates. Garnish with reserved hearts of palm and tomato wedges.

6 servings

Chicken-Tortellini Salad with Basil Dressing

INGREDIENTS

- 2 *Gold Kist Farms* boneless, skinless, split chicken breasts (about 1 pound)
- 1/4 cup chicken broth or water
- 1 package (12 ounces) cheese-filled tortellini
- 1 jar (4½ ounces) marinated artichoke hearts, drained and coarsely chopped
- 1 small red onion, thinly sliced

DRESSING

- 1/3 cup white wine vinegar
- 1/4 cup packed fresh basil
- 2 tablespoons sugar
- 1/4 teaspoon minced garlic
- Salt and freshly ground pepper to taste
- 1/2 cup olive oil, extra virgin preferred

❖ ❖ ❖ ❖

- Lettuce leaves to serve (optional)

Place chicken breasts in single layer in microproof pie plate with thickest part of chicken at outer edge of dish. Add chicken broth, cover, and microcook on HIGH about 6 minutes or until chicken is no longer pink inside. Cool and cut into bite-size pieces. Place in large bowl and set aside.

Cook tortellini according to package directions. Rinse under cold water to stop cooking and drain. Add to chicken with artichoke hearts and onion. Toss gently and set aside.

To make dressing, place vinegar, basil, sugar, garlic, salt, and pepper in food processor or blender and process until smooth. Add olive oil very slowly with machine running. Pour dressing over chicken mixture and toss gently to coat. Serve at room temperature or cover and refrigerate until ready to serve.

To serve, line salad bowl or serving plates with lettuce and spoon salad into center of bowl or onto plates.

4 to 6 servings

Variation: Place chicken breasts in single layer in saucepan and add enough chicken broth or water to cover by ½ inch. Bring to a boil, reduce heat, cover, and poach 12 to 15 minutes or until chicken is no longer pink inside. Drain, cut into bite-size pieces, and proceed as above.

Chicken-Tortellini Salad with Basil Dressing, **facing page**

Chicken-Pasta Salad

INGREDIENTS

2 *Gold Kist Farms* boneless, skinless, split chicken breasts (about 1 pound)
8 ounces (half of 16-ounce package) rotini pasta, cooked, drained, and cooled
About 24 broccoli flowerets, steamed and cooled
2 medium-size tomatoes, cut into small wedges
1 small onion, thinly sliced
½ green and/or red bell pepper, thinly sliced
1 can (6 ounces) pitted black olives, cut in half
4 tablespoons grated Parmesan cheese

DRESSING

3 tablespoons red wine vinegar
2 tablespoons Dijon-style mustard
¼ cup olive oil
¼ cup vegetable oil
¼ teaspoon dried basil
¼ teaspoon dried oregano
Salt and freshly ground pepper to taste

❖ ❖ ❖ ❖

Crusty warm French or Italian bread to serve

Place chicken in single layer in saucepan. Add enough water to cover by ½ inch. Bring to a boil, reduce heat, cover, and poach 12 to 15 minutes or until chicken is no longer pink inside. Drain, cool, and cut into bite-size pieces. Place in large serving bowl. Add pasta, broccoli, tomatoes, onion, green pepper, olives, and Parmesan cheese. Toss gently and set aside.

To make dressing, place vinegar and mustard in blender or food processor and process briefly to combine. Combine oils in 1-cup measuring cup and add slowly with machine running until thoroughly combined. Add 3 tablespoons water and seasonings and process briefly. Drizzle dressing over salad and toss gently. Adjust seasoning if necessary, cover, and refrigerate at least 2 hours, preferably overnight.

Serve with crusty bread.

4 to 6 servings

Variation: Other vegetables or different pasta shapes may be substituted for those suggested above.

Chicken-Guacamole Salad with Cilantro

INGREDIENTS

- 3 to 4 *Gold Kist Farms* boneless, skinless, split chicken breasts (about 2 pounds)
- 1¼ cups chopped onion
- 1 cup chopped celery
- 1 cup chopped red or green bell pepper
- 1 cup loosely packed chopped fresh cilantro
- 4 ripe avocados, pitted and peeled
- Juice of ½ lime, about 1 tablespoon
- 1 cup mayonnaise
- 3 to 4 jalapeño peppers, seeded and minced (optional)
- 2 teaspoons ground cumin
- ¼ teaspoon garlic powder or to taste
- Salt and freshly ground pepper to taste
- Lettuce leaves to serve (optional)
- Fresh cilantro leaves to garnish (optional)

Note: If desired, prepare chicken mixture ahead of time, cover, and refrigerate. Avocado mixture should be prepared shortly before serving. Recipe can be cut in half, if desired.

Place chicken in single layer in large saucepan. Add enough water to cover by ½ inch. Bring to a boil, reduce heat, cover, and poach 12 to 15 minutes or until chicken is no longer pink inside. Drain, cool, and cut into bite-size pieces.

Place chicken in large bowl. Add onion, celery, bell pepper, and cilantro. Toss gently and set aside.

Cut avocados into small pieces and place in separate bowl. Mash coarsely, leaving some small chunks. Stir in lime juice. Add mayonnaise, jalapeño peppers, cumin, garlic powder, salt, and pepper. Stir until well combined and add to chicken mixture. Stir gently and serve immediately.

To serve, line salad bowl with lettuce leaves and spoon salad into center of bowl. Garnish with cilantro leaves, if desired.

8 to 10 servings

Variations: Fill pita pockets with chicken salad and top with chopped tomatoes and alfafa sprouts, or roll in hot flour tortillas and add your favorite toppings.

Chicken-Apricot Salad

INGREDIENTS

- 2 *Gold Kist Farms* boneless, skinless, split chicken breasts (about 1 pound)
- 1/4 cup chicken broth or water
- 1/2 cup light or regular mayonnaise
- 1/2 cup plain low-fat or regular yogurt
- 2 teaspoons Dijon-style mustard
- 1/2 teaspoon chicken bouillon granules
- 1/2 teaspoon curry powder
- 1 1/2 cups chopped dried apricots
- 1 cup chopped celery
- 1/3 cup thinly sliced scallions (green onions), green tops included
- Salt and white pepper to taste
- 1/2 cup chopped walnuts or pecans
- Lettuce leaves to serve (optional)

Place chicken breasts in single layer in microproof pie plate with thickest part of chicken at outer edge of dish. Add chicken broth, cover, and microcook on HIGH about 6 minutes or until chicken is no longer pink inside. Cool and cut into chunks. Place in large bowl and set aside.

Place mayonnaise in small bowl. Stir in yogurt, mustard, bouillon, and curry powder. Stir into chicken. Add apricots, celery, scallions, salt, and pepper. Walnuts can be stirred into salad or sprinkled on top as garnish.

To serve, line salad bowl with lettuce and spoon salad into center of bowl.

6 servings

Variations: Place chicken breasts in single layer in large saucepan with enough chicken broth or water to cover by 1/2 inch. Bring to a boil, reduce heat, cover, and poach 12 to 15 minutes or until chicken is no longer pink inside. Drain, cut into chunks, and proceed as above. Boneless, skinless chicken thighs may be substituted for chicken breasts. To reduce calories, substitute orange sections for apricots and omit nuts.

Chicken-Apricot Salad, facing page

Sopa de Pollo y Frijoles (Chicken and Bean Soup)

INGREDIENTS

- 3 to 4 *Gold Kist Farms* boneless, skinless, split chicken breasts (about 2 pounds)
- 3 cans (14½ ounces each) chicken broth (about 5½ cups)
- 5 to 6 tablespoons vegetable oil, divided
- 1 large onion, chopped
- 4 medium-size jalapeño peppers, seeded and chopped
- 2 cloves garlic, minced
- 1 tablespoon chili powder
- 1 can (14½ ounces) tomatoes, chopped and liquid reserved
- 2 cans (15 ounces each) pinto beans, drained and rinsed
- Salt and freshly ground pepper to taste
- 6 corn tortillas (7 inches each) cut into ¼ to ½-inch strips
- ¾ cup (3 ounces) shredded sharp Cheddar cheese
- ⅓ cup dairy sour cream
- 3 tablespoons finely chopped fresh cilantro

Place chicken and chicken broth in large saucepan or stockpot. Bring to a boil, reduce heat, cover, and poach 12 to 15 minutes or until chicken is no longer pink inside. Remove chicken to plate, leaving broth in saucepan, and set both aside.

Heat 2 tablespoons oil in medium-size skillet. Add onion and jalapeño peppers. Cook, stirring occasionally, about 3 minutes. Add garlic and cook until onion is transparent. Stir in chili powder. Add vegetables to saucepan with reserved broth and stir in tomatoes with liquid, beans, salt, and pepper. Shred or chop cooked chicken and add to soup. Bring to a boil, reduce heat, cover, and simmer 20 minutes. Remove from heat and set aside to cool. Pour into large container, cover, and refrigerate 3 to 4 hours or overnight to blend flavors. Reheat soup just before serving.

Before serving, heat remaining 3 to 4 tablespoons oil in skillet. Add tortilla strips and cook until crisp. Drain on paper towels and season with salt, if desired.

To serve, divide cheese and tortilla strips in 6 soup bowls and ladle soup over. Garnish with dollop of sour cream and sprinkle with cilantro. Alternatively, place cheese, tortilla strips, sour cream, and cilantro in separate serving bowls and pass at table.

6 servings

Wild and Creamy Chicken-Rice Soup

INGREDIENTS

- 3 to 4 *Gold Kist Farms* boneless, skinless, split chicken breasts (about 2 pounds)
- 3 cans (14½ ounces each) chicken broth (about 5½ cups)
- 1 package (6 ounces) long grain and wild rice with seasoning packet
- ½ cup thinly sliced scallions (green onions), green tops included
- About 12 broccoli flowerets
- 1 carrot, cut in julienne strips
- ½ cup (1 stick) butter or margarine
- ½ cup all-purpose flour
- Salt and freshly ground pepper to taste
- 2 cups milk or half and half
- 8 slices bacon, cooked and crumbled
- 1 tablespoon chopped pimiento
- ¼ cup dry sherry, dry white wine, or white cooking wine
- 1 tablespoon chopped fresh chives to garnish
- Crusty hot bread or muffins to serve

Place chicken in saucepan in single layer. Add enough water to cover by ½ inch. Bring to a boil, reduce heat, cover, and poach 12 to 15 minutes or until chicken is no longer pink inside. Drain, reserving ½ cup cooking liquid, and set chicken aside until cool enough to handle. Cut into bite-size pieces and set aside.

Place chicken broth, reserved cooking broth, rice, seasoning packet, and scallions in large saucepan or stockpot. Bring to a boil, reduce heat, cover, and simmer 30 minutes. Add broccoli and carrots and simmer 10 minutes.

Melt butter in medium-size saucepan. Stir in flour slowly and season with salt and pepper. Cook 2 minutes, stirring constantly. Add milk gradually and cook, stirring constantly until thickened and smooth. Stir milk mixture into rice mixture slowly. Add chicken, crumbled bacon, pimiento, and wine. Heat gently, stirring. Do not boil. If soup is too thick, add desired amount additional broth or milk.

To serve, spoon into soup bowls and garnish with chives. Serve with crusty bread or muffins.

4 to 6 servings

Festival Chicken Soup

INGREDIENTS

- 2 *Gold Kist Farms* boneless, skinless, split chicken breasts (about 1 pound)
- 6 cups chicken broth, divided
- About 2 tablespoons vegetable oil
- 1 cup thinly sliced carrot
- 1 cup thinly sliced celery
- 1 cup chopped onion
- 2 cloves garlic, minced
- 1½ cups thick, chunky salsa
- ½ cup rice
- ½ small zucchini, sliced
- 1 cup whole-kernel corn
- 4 corn tortillas (7 inches each), to serve (optional)
- Oil for brushing
- 1 cup (4 ounces) shredded Cheddar cheese to serve
- ½ cup thinly sliced scallions (green onions), green tops included, to serve

Place chicken in single layer in saucepan. Add 1 cup chicken broth, bring to a boil, reduce heat, cover, and poach 12 to 15 minutes or until chicken is no longer pink inside. Remove chicken, reserving broth, and cut chicken into bite-size pieces. Set aside.

Heat oil in large saucepan or stockpot. Add carrot, celery, and onion. Cook over medium heat until onion is transparent, about 3 minutes. Add garlic and cook 2 minutes. Pour in reserved cooking broth, remaining 5 cups chicken broth, and salsa. Bring to a boil and add rice and zucchini. Reduce heat, cover, and simmer until vegetables and rice are almost tender, about 20 minutes. Add corn and reserved chicken to saucepan, cover, and simmer until rice is fully cooked, about 5 to 10 minutes.

Preheat oven to 400°F.

Brush tortillas lightly with oil and cut into ¼-inch strips. Spread on large baking sheet and bake until golden brown and crisp, stirring frequently, 10 to 15 minutes. Remove from oven.

To serve, ladle soup into shallow soup bowls and top each serving with 2 tablespoons cheese, scallions, and tortilla strips, if desired.

8 servings

▲ Festival Chicken Soup, facing page

▼ Southwestern-Style Chicken Sandwiches, page 82

Chicken Pitas

INGREDIENTS

2 *Gold Kist Farms* boneless, skinless, split chicken breasts (about 1 pound), cut into bite-size pieces
1/4 cup chicken broth or water
1 medium-size onion, chopped
2 cloves garlic, minced
1 tablespoon chopped fresh tarragon or 1 teaspoon dried tarragon
1/2 pound fresh mushrooms, sliced
1/3 cup plain low-fat or regular yogurt
1/3 cup light or regular mayonnaise
1/2 cup chopped celery
1/4 cup thinly sliced scallions (green onions), green tops included
Salt and freshly ground pepper to taste
6 pita breads (6 inches each), cut in half crosswise to form 12 pockets
6 ounces (half of 12-ounce package) spinach leaves, washed and dried

Place chicken in microproof 2-quart casserole. Add chicken broth, onion, and garlic. Sprinkle with tarragon. Cover and microcook on HIGH about 3 minutes. Add mushrooms and stir gently. Cover and microcook on HIGH about 3 minutes or until chicken is no longer pink inside. Drain, if necessary, and stir in yogurt, mayonnaise, celery, scallions, salt, and pepper.

To serve, line pita pockets with spinach leaves and fill with chicken mixture.

6 servings

Variation: Eliminate chicken broth and substitute 2 tablespoons olive oil. Heat in large skillet. Add chicken and onion and cook 5 minutes. Stir in garlic, tarragon, and mushrooms. Cook, stirring, 4 to 5 minutes. Spoon chicken mixture into bowl with slotted spoon and proceed as above.

▲ Chicken Pitas, facing page

▼ Chicken Alfredo, page 86

Chicken Alfredo

INGREDIENTS

- 4 tablespoons olive oil, butter, or margarine
- 6 to 8 *Gold Kist Farms* boneless, skinless chicken thighs (about 1½ pounds), cut into bite-size pieces
- ⅓ cup thinly sliced scallions (green onions), green tops included
- 1 teaspoon minced garlic
- 8 ounces (half of 16-ounce package) hot, cooked fettuccine
- 2 eggs
- 1 cup half and half
- ½ cup grated Parmesan cheese
- ¼ cup minced fresh parsley
- Salt and freshly ground pepper to taste

Note: For more lightly sauced dish, double amount of pasta.

Heat oil in large skillet, add chicken, and cook 10 to 15 minutes or until fork-tender, opaque, and juices run clear. Add scallions and garlic and cook 2 to 3 minutes. Remove from heat and stir in cooked fettuccine.

Place eggs in small bowl and beat lightly. Add half and half and cheese and beat until well combined. Stir into chicken mixture slowly and cook over medium heat 3 to 4 minutes or until heated through. Do not boil. Stir in parsley, salt, and pepper.

Place in large serving bowl and serve immediately with extra Parmesan cheese, if desired.

4 to 6 servings

Chicken Fajita Pizza

INGREDIENTS

1 can (10 ounces) refrigerated pizza dough
2 tablespoons olive oil
1 small onion, sliced
½ red bell pepper, cut into thin strips
½ green bell pepper, cut into thin strips
2 *Gold Kist Farms* boneless, skinless, split chicken breasts (about 1 pound), cut into bite-size pieces
3 cloves garlic or to taste, crushed
2 teaspoons ground cumin
1 teaspoon cayenne
1 can (8 ounces) refried beans
1 jar (16 ounces) chunky salsa
2 ounces (half of 4-ounce can) chopped jalapeño peppers (optional)
1 cup (4 ounces) shredded mozzarella cheese
Dairy sour cream and guacamole to serve (optional)

Preheat oven to 425° F. Lightly grease 14-inch pizza pan and set aside.

Roll out pizza dough to 15-inch circle and fit into prepared pan. Prick bottom with fork and bake in preheated oven 8 to 10 minutes or until lightly browned. Remove from oven and set aside. Do not turn oven off.

Heat oil in large skillet. Add onion and bell peppers and stir-fry 3 minutes. Add chicken and stir-fry 5 minutes. Stir in garlic, cumin, and cayenne. Stir-fry 3 to 5 minutes or until chicken is no longer pink inside.

Spread refried beans on pizza crust, top with salsa, chicken mixture, and jalapeño peppers. Sprinkle with cheese and bake in preheated oven 3 to 5 minutes or until cheese is melted.

To serve, cut into 8 wedges and serve with sour cream and guacamole, if desired.

4 servings

Chicken-Rice Pilaf

INGREDIENTS

- 1 package (6 ounces) long grain and wild rice with seasoning packet
- 1 can (14½ ounces) chicken broth
- ½ cup golden or black raisins
- 2 tablespoons olive oil
- 1 *Gold Kist Farms* boneless, skinless, split chicken breast (about ½ pound), cut into ½-inch strips
- 1 cup chopped celery
- ½ cup thinly sliced scallions (green onions), green tops included
- ½ cup coarsely chopped pecans
- Salt and freshly ground pepper to taste

Variation: Substitute boneless, skinless chicken thighs for chicken breasts, if desired.

Cook rice according to package directions, substituting chicken broth and ½ cup water for water called for on package. When rice is done, stir in raisins, cover, and let stand 10 minutes.

Heat oil in large skillet and stir-fry chicken strips 3 to 4 minutes. Add celery, scallions, and pecans and stir-fry until celery is crisp-tender and chicken is no longer pink inside. Add chicken mixture to rice and season with salt and pepper.

To serve, spoon into serving bowl and serve hot or at room temperature.

6 servings

Chicken Rice Pilaf, **facing page**

GRILLING

Mesquite Chicken Fajitas, page 97

Chicken Kabobs

INGREDIENTS

1½ pounds *Gold Kist Farms* boneless, skinless, split chicken breasts (2 to 3) or thighs (6 to 8)

MARINADE

½ cup pineapple juice from 16-ounce can pineapple chunks, chunks reserved
⅓ cup cider vinegar
1 tablespoon vegetable oil
3 tablespoons light brown sugar
3 tablespoons soy sauce
2 to 3 cloves garlic, minced
1 tablespoon grated fresh ginger or 1 teaspoon ground ginger
1 teaspoon freshly ground black pepper
¼ cup chopped fresh parsley

❖ ❖ ❖ ❖

1 can (16 ounces) pineapple chunks
1 medium-size red bell pepper, cut into 1½-inch chunks
1 medium-size green bell pepper, cut into 1½-inch chunks

Cut chicken into 1½-inch pieces and place in non-metallic baking dish or resealable plastic bag. Set aside.

To make marinade, place marinade ingredients in 2-cup measuring cup and beat with whisk until well combined. Pour over chicken and cover or close bag. Refrigerate several hours or overnight.

Preheat grill and lightly coat with oil or cooking spray.

Drain chicken and discard marinade. Thread chicken pieces on skewers alternating with pineapple and pepper chunks. When grill is ready, place filled skewers on prepared grill 4 to 6 inches from source of heat. Cook 10 to 12 minutes or until meat is no longer pink inside. Turn at least once during cooking.

4 to 6 servings

▲ Chicken Kabobs, facing page ▼ Mesquite Chicken Burgers with Chutney, page 94

Mesquite Chicken Burgers with Chutney

INGREDIENTS

- 1 pound *Gold Kist Farms* boneless, skinless chicken thighs (5 to 6) or split breasts (about 2), ground (see Note)
- ½ pound bulk pork sausage, spicy or hot
- 1¼ teaspoons mesquite seasoning salt, or to taste

CHUTNEY

- ¾ cup apricot preserves
- 2 tablespoons balsamic vinegar
- 1 tablespoon Dijon-style mustard
- 1 teaspoon grated fresh ginger or ¼ teaspoon ground ginger
- 1 teaspoon minced garlic
- 1 teaspoon minced fresh thyme or ¼ teaspoon dried thyme
- ¼ cup finely chopped red bell pepper
- ¼ cup finely chopped sweet onion
- 2 teaspoons finely chopped jalapeño pepper or to taste

❖ ❖ ❖ ❖

- 4 Kaiser or onion rolls to serve
- Dijon-style mustard to serve

Place chicken, sausage, and mesquite salt in bowl and stir to combine. Shape into 4 patties, cover, and place in refrigerator at least 20 minutes to chill.

To make chutney, place preserves, vinegar, mustard, ginger, and garlic in small saucepan. Stir to combine and simmer over low heat about 3 minutes. Remove from heat and stir in thyme, red pepper, onion, and jalapeño pepper. Set aside.

Preheat grill and lightly coat with oil or cooking spray.

Place burgers on grill 4 to 6 inches from source of heat. Cook, turning as needed, until juices run clear, about 10 to 12 minutes per side, depending on thickness of burger. Lightly toast rolls on grill and spread with mustard. Serve with chutney.

4 servings

Note: Have butcher grind chicken or process at home in meat grinder or food processor. Burgers may also be broiled in oven broiler or sautéed in skillet. Chicken breasts can be substituted for thighs. However, thighs are more flavorful and juicy than breasts when used in burger mixture.

Grilled Margarita Sandwiches

INGREDIENTS

4 *Gold Kist Farms* boneless, skinless, split chicken breasts

MARINADE

½ cup lime juice
½ cup Triple Sec
2 tablespoons soy sauce
6 slices fresh ginger or 1 teaspoon ground ginger

❖ ❖ ❖ ❖

1 tablespoon cornstarch
4 slices Monterey Jack cheese
Chutney or honey-mustard to serve (optional)
4 Kaiser rolls to serve

Place chicken breasts between sheets of plastic wrap and pound with meat mallet to even thickness. Place in single layer in large non-metallic dish or resealable plastic bag. Place lime juice, Triple Sec, soy sauce, and ¼ cup water in 2-cup measuring cup and beat with whisk until well combined. Stir in ginger. Pour over chicken, cover or close bag, and refrigerate 1 to 3 hours, turning at least once.

Preheat grill and lightly coat with oil or cooking spray.

Remove chicken from marinade and set chicken aside. Place cornstarch in 2-cup measuring cup. Add small amount of marinade and stir to smooth paste. Add remainder of marinade and stir. Pour into small saucepan and bring to a boil. Reduce heat and cook, stirring, over moderate heat until slightly thickened, forming a glaze. Remove fresh ginger and discard. Cover saucepan to keep marinade warm and set aside off heat.

Place chicken breasts on prepared grill 4 to 6 inches from source of heat. Cook 4 minutes on each side. Brush both sides of chicken with glaze and cook 2 to 3 minutes on each side or until chicken is no longer pink inside. Place 1 slice of cheese on top of each breast and cook 1 minute to melt cheese.

To serve, spread chutney or honey-mustard on inside of each roll and place chicken breast on roll.

4 servings

Patio Chicken Paella

RICE PILAF

- 3 cups rice
- 3 cans (14½ ounces each) chicken broth
- 2 tablespoons olive oil
- 2 cans (14½ ounces each) stewed tomatoes, chopped, liquid reserved
- ½ cup dry sherry
- 1 onion, chopped
- 4 cloves garlic, minced
- ½ teaspoon ground coriander
- ½ teaspoon saffron
- ½ teaspoon dried oregano
- 1 bay leaf
- 1 dozen little neck clams, soaked and scrubbed (optional)
- 2 cups frozen peas
- 1 can (16 ounces) black beans, drained and rinsed

TO GRILL

- 8 *Gold Kist Farms* boneless, skinless, split chicken breasts (about 4 pounds)
- 1 pound (about 21 to 30) large shrimp, peeled
- 1 red bell pepper, cut into strips
- 1 green bell pepper, cut into strips
- Olive oil for basting
- ½ teaspoon ground coriander
- Salt and freshly ground pepper to taste
- ½ pound fully cooked smoked sausage

❖ ❖ ❖ ❖

- 1 to 1½ pounds cooked asparagus to serve
- 1 to 2 tablespoons drained capers to garnish
- ⅓ cup sliced, pitted black or green olives to garnish

Preheat oven to 350°F.

To make pilaf, place rice, chicken broth, 2 tablespoons oil, tomatoes with their liquid, sherry, onion, garlic, ½ teaspoon coriander, saffron, oregano, and bay leaf in 4-quart casserole. Cover and bake in preheated oven 30 to 40 minutes or until rice is tender. (There will be some liquid left.) Stir in clams, if desired, peas, and beans. Cook 5 minutes or until clams open. Discard any clams that do not open and remove and discard bay leaf. Season with salt and pepper. Set aside and keep warm until ready to serve.

Preheat grill and lightly coat grill and grill basket with oil or cooking spray.

While pilaf is baking, place chicken, shrimp, and pepper strips in separate dishes and brush lightly with olive oil. Sprinkle with ½ teaspoon coriander, and season generously with salt and pepper. Let stand 15 to 20 minutes.

To grill, place shrimp and pepper strips in prepared grill basket and set aside. Place chicken on prepared grill 4 to 6 inches from source of heat. Cook about 5 minutes on each side. Add sausage and filled grill basket to grill. Cook sausage just until heated through. Cook shrimp, peppers, and chicken about 5 minutes, turning frequently and brushing occasionally with oil, until shrimp are pink, pepper strips crisp-tender, and chicken is no longer pink inside. (Do not overcook.) Cut cooked chicken breasts into ½-inch strips and cooked sausage into 1-inch chunks.

To serve, fluff rice and arrange chicken, shrimp, sausage, peppers, and asparagus over rice. Garnish with capers and olives.

8 to 10 servings

Mesquite Chicken Fajitas

INGREDIENTS

6 *Gold Kist Farms* boneless, skinless, split chicken breasts
3 bell peppers (red, yellow, and green), cut into ¼ to ½-inch strips
1 medium-size red onion, cut into ¼ to ½-inch slices

MARINADE

1 bottle (12 ounces) mesquite marinade
3 tablespoons peanut oil
1 teaspoon chili powder

SAUCE

½ cup lime juice
¼ cup honey
2 tablespoons peanut oil
2 tablespoons balsamic vinegar
2 tablespoons coarse-grain mustard
2 tablespoons finely chopped fresh cilantro
1 tablespoon minced chipotle pepper in adobo sauce or minced jalapeño peppers
1 teaspoon minced garlic
1 teaspoon ground cumin
Freshly ground pepper to taste

❖ ❖ ❖ ❖

12 flour tortillas (7 inches each), wrapped in foil and warmed on grill
Dairy sour cream to serve (optional)

Place chicken, peppers, and onion in large non-metallic bowl or resealable plastic bag. Place marinade ingredients in 4-cup measuring cup and beat with whisk until well combined. Pour over chicken mixture, cover or close bag, and refrigerate at least 1 hour, turning several times.

Place sauce ingredients in 2-cup measuring cup and beat with whisk until well combined. Set aside.

Preheat grill and lightly coat grill and grill basket with oil or cooking spray.

Remove chicken and vegetables from marinade with slotted spoon and set aside. Pour marinade into saucepan and bring to a boil. Set aside.

Place vegetables in prepared grill basket 4 to 6 inches from source of heat. Cook just until crisp-tender, about 5 minutes. Place chicken on prepared grill and cook about 10 to 12 minutes, or until chicken is no longer pink inside. Baste frequently with cooked marinade. Slice chicken diagonally into strips.

Divide chicken and vegetables among warm tortillas, drizzle with reserved sauce, and top with sour cream, if desired. Roll up to enclose filling or allow guests to make their own fajitas. Serve immediately.

6 servings

Chicken Premo

INGREDIENTS

4 *Gold Kist Farms* boneless, skinless, split chicken breasts
2 tablespoons butter, melted (preferably no substitution)
Cajun spice to taste

SAUCE

¼ pound (1 stick) butter or margarine
2 tablespoons minced garlic
⅓ cup finely chopped fresh cilantro
5 tablespoons yellow mustard

❖ ❖ ❖ ❖

4 slices Jarlsberg cheese

Dip chicken breasts in melted butter, lightly sprinkle both sides with Cajun spice, and set aside.

Preheat grill and lightly coat with oil or cooking spray.

To prepare sauce, melt butter in a small saucepan. Add garlic and cook over medium heat 2 minutes. Add cilantro and cook 2 minutes. Remove from heat and stir in mustard. Set aside.

Place chicken on prepared grill 4 to 6 inches from source of heat. Baste with sauce and cook 12 to 15 minutes or until chicken is no longer pink inside. Turn chicken and baste with sauce frequently during cooking. Place cheese slice on each breast and baste with additional sauce. Cook just until cheese begins to melt. Serve immediately.

4 servings

Honey Grilled Chicken Breasts

INGREDIENTS

4 *Gold Kist Farms* boneless, skinless, split chicken breasts

BASTING SAUCE

1 tablespoon butter, melted or 1 tablespoon vegetable oil
1/4 cup honey
1/4 cup yellow mustard
1 tablespoon lemon juice
Salt and freshly ground pepper to taste

Place chicken breasts between sheets of plastic wrap and flatten with meat mallet to uniform thickness. Set aside.

Preheat grill and lightly coat with oil or cooking spray.

Place sauce ingredients in small bowl and beat until well combined. Set aside.

When grill is ready, place chicken on prepared grill 4 to 6 inches from source of heat. Cook 7 minutes, turning several times. Brush both sides of breasts with honey mixture and grill 7 to 10 minutes or until chicken is no longer pink inside.

4 servings

Grilled Peppercorn Chicken

INGREDIENTS

4 *Gold Kist Farms* boneless, skinless, split chicken breasts or 6 to 8 boneless, skinless thighs (about 1½ to 2 pounds)

MARINADE

½ tablespoon black peppercorns
5 tablespoons soy sauce
2 tablespoons dry sherry
4 cloves garlic

Place chicken between sheets of plastic wrap and flatten with meat mallet to even thickness. Place in single layer in non-metallic dish or resealable plastic bag and set aside.

Place peppercorns in food processor or blender and process several seconds. Add remaining marinade ingredients and process to combine. Pour over chicken, cover or close bag, and refrigerate several hours or overnight, turning occasionally.

Preheat grill and lightly coat with oil or cooking spray.

Remove chicken from marinade and discard marinade. When grill is ready, place chicken on prepared grill 4 to 6 inches from source of heat. Cook 12 to 15 minutes, turning several times, or until breasts are no longer pink inside or thighs are opaque. (If using smoker, cook 30 to 40 minutes, turning after first 20 minutes.)

4 to 6 servings

Oriental-Style Grilled Chicken

INGREDIENTS

- 3 to 3½ pound *Gold Kist Farms* whole chicken, cut up or chicken parts of choice

MARINADE

- 1 cup soy sauce
- ½ cup firmly packed brown sugar
- ¼ cup grated fresh ginger or 2 teaspoons ground ginger
- 1 tablespoon dry mustard
- 3 cloves garlic, minced

Place chicken pieces in single layer in large non-metallic casserole and set aside.

Place soy sauce, brown sugar, ginger, mustard, and garlic in small bowl and stir until well combined. Pour over chicken, cover, and place in refrigerator at least 1 hour or overnight, turning occasionally.

Drain marinade from chicken, place in small saucepan, and bring to a boil. Set cooked marinade aside to use for basting.

Preheat grill and lightly coat with oil or cooking spray.

Arrange chicken in casserole with thickest parts at outer edge of dish. Cover and microcook on HIGH 10 minutes. Turn chicken, cover, and microcook 5 minutes. Place chicken on prepared grill and cook 10 to 15 minutes, turning and basting frequently with cooked marinade, until temperature on meat thermometer is 170°F and juices run clear when thighs are pierced with fork.

4 servings

Tuscan Grilled Chicken

INGREDIENTS

3 to 3½ pound *Gold Kist Farms* whole chicken, cut up or chicken parts of choice

MARINADE

- Juice of 1 lemon
- ½ cup dry red wine
- 1 tablespoon brandy
- 5 tablespoons olive oil
- 1 clove garlic, crushed
- 2 to 3 sprigs fresh rosemary or ½ teaspoon dried rosemary
- Salt and freshly ground pepper to taste

Place chicken pieces in single layer in large non-metallic dish or resealable plastic bag.

Place lemon juice, red wine, and brandy in 2-cup measuring cup and beat with whisk to combine. Beat in olive oil. Add remaining ingredients and beat. Pour over chicken and cover or close bag. Place in refrigerator to chill several hours or overnight.

Preheat grill and lightly coat with oil or cooking spray.

Remove chicken from marinade and discard marinade. When grill is ready, place chicken, skin-side up, on prepared grill 4 to 6 inches from source of heat. Cook 35 to 45 minutes or until temperature on meat thermometer is 170°F and juices run clear when thighs are pierced with fork. Turn chicken every 10 minutes during cooking.

4 servings

Carolina Barbecued Chicken

INGREDIENTS

4 to 6 pounds *Gold Kist Farms* chicken parts of choice, or 4 to 6 boneless, skinless, split chicken breasts, or 4 Cornish Hens, split lengthwise

BASTING SAUCE

- ½ cup (1 stick) butter or margarine, cut into chunks
- ¼ cup cider vinegar
- ¼ cup sugar
- ¼ cup yellow mustard
- 1 tablespoon Worcestershire sauce
- 2 teaspoons freshly ground black pepper, or to taste
- ½ teaspoon cayenne (optional)

Preheat grill and lightly coat with oil or cooking spray. Rinse chicken pieces, pat dry, and set aside.

Place butter in 2-cup microproof measuring cup. Microcook on HIGH 2 minutes or until butter is melted. Stir in vinegar, sugar, mustard, Worcestershire, pepper, and cayenne. Alternatively, place ingredients in saucepan and heat until butter is melted. Stir to combine.

Place chicken on prepared grill 4 to 6 inches from source of heat, basting and turning frequently. Cook bone-in pieces 35 to 45 minutes, depending on size, and boneless pieces 12 to 15 minutes.

Chicken is done when no longer pink inside and juices run clear when thighs are pierced with fork. Bone-in pieces are done when temperature on meat thermometer is 170°F.

4 to 6 servings

Grilled Cornish Hens

INGREDIENTS

4 *Gold Kist Farms* Cornish Hens (1 pound 6 ounces each)

MARINADE

1 cup orange juice
½ cup vegetable oil
2 tablespoons soy sauce
3 cloves garlic, minced
1 tablespoon chopped fresh ginger or 1 teaspoon ground ginger

❖ ❖ ❖ ❖

Salt and freshly ground pepper to taste

Remove giblets and reserve for use another time. Split hens lengthwise, rinse, and pat dry.

Place hens in single layer in large non-metallic dish or resealable plastic bag. Place marinade ingredients in 2-cup measuring cup and beat with whisk until well combined. Pour marinade over, cover or close bag, and refrigerate several hours or overnight.

Preheat grill and lightly coat with oil or cooking spray.

Remove hens from marinade and season with salt and pepper. Pour marinade into saucepan and bring to a boil. Set cooked marinade aside to use for basting.

When grill is ready, place hens, skin-side up, on prepared grill, 4 to 6 inches from source of heat. Brush with cooked marinade and cook 25 to 35 minutes, turning and basting often with marinade. Cook until temperature on meat thermometer is 170° F and juices run clear when thighs are pierced with fork.

6 to 8 servings

Grilled Cornish Hens,
facing page

Grilled Cornish Hens with Wild Rice Salad

INGREDIENTS

4 *Gold Kist Farms* Cornish Hens (1 pound 6 ounces each)

MARINADE

½ cup soy sauce
½ cup vegetable oil
½ cup bourbon
1 tablespoon grated fresh ginger or 1 teaspoon ground ginger
1 large onion, thinly sliced

SALAD

1 package (6 ounces) long grain and wild rice with seasoning packet
1 can (14½ ounces) chicken broth
½ teaspoon curry powder
1 bottle (8 ounces) vinaigrette dressing, divided
1 can (8 ounces) sliced water chestnuts, drained
1 jar (6 ounces) marinated artichokes, quartered, liquid reserved
5 scallions (green onions), thinly sliced

❖ ❖ ❖ ❖

Tomato wedges, orange slices, and purple grapes to garnish (optional)

Variation: Hens may be roasted on rack in preheated 350° F oven. Baste frequently with cooked marinade and roast about 1 hour 15 minutes or until hens test done as in recipe.

Remove giblets and reserve for use another time. Rinse hens and pat dry.

Place hens in single layer in large non-metallic dish or resealable plastic bag. Place marinade ingredients in 2-cup measuring cup and beat with whisk until well combined. Pour marinade over hens, cover or close bag, and refrigerate several hours or overnight.

To prepare salad, place rice, seasoning packet, broth plus enough water to measure 2⅓ cups, and curry powder in saucepan. Stir to combine, cover, and cook according to package directions. Set aside to cool. When cool, stir in ½ cup vinaigrette dressing, water chestnuts, artichokes with their liquid, and scallions. Cover and refrigerate several hours or overnight.

Preheat grill and lightly coat with oil or cooking spray. Remove hens from marinade, pour marinade into saucepan, and bring to a boil. Set cooked marinade aside to use for basting.

When grill is ready, place hens on grill 4 to 6 inches from source of heat and brush with cooked marinade. Cook 45 to 55 minutes, turning and basting often with marinade, until temperature on meat thermometer is 180° F and juices run clear when thighs are pierced with fork.

To serve, spoon rice salad onto large serving platter and arrange hens over rice. If desired, garnish with tomato wedges, orange slices, and purple grapes. Pass reserved ½ cup vinaigrette dressing at table.

4 to 6 servings

Grilled Cornish Hens with
Wild Rice Salad, facing page

Gingered Barbecued Cornish Hens

INGREDIENTS

4 *Gold Kist Farms* Cornish Hens (1 pound 6 ounces each)

MARINADE

1 cup ketchup
6 tablespoons Worcestershire sauce
4 tablespoons peanut oil
2 tablespoons honey
1 tablespoon grated fresh ginger or 1 teaspoon ground ginger
1 large clove garlic, minced
1 teaspoon dry mustard
1 teaspoon chili powder

❖ ❖ ❖ ❖

Salt and freshly ground pepper to taste

Remove giblets and reserve for use another time. Split hens lengthwise, rinse, and pat dry.

Place hens in single layer in large non-metallic dish or resealable plastic bag. Place marinade ingredients in 2-cup measuring cup and beat with whisk until well combined. Pour marinade over hens, cover or close bag, and refrigerate several hours or overnight.

Preheat grill and lightly coat with oil or cooking spray.

Remove hens from marinade and season with salt and pepper. Pour marinade into saucepan and bring to a boil. Set cooked marinade aside to use for basting.

When grill is ready, place hens, skin-side up, on prepared grill 4 to 6 inches from source of heat. Brush with cooked marinade and cook 25 to 35 minutes, turning and basting often with marinade. Cook until temperature on meat thermometer is 170° F and juices run clear when thighs are pierced with fork.

4 to 6 servings

Grilled Cornish Hens with Herb Butter

INGREDIENTS

4 *Gold Kist Farms* Cornish Hens (1 pound 6 ounces each)
Salt and freshly ground pepper to taste

HERB BUTTERS
(choose one)

Tarragon Butter

8 tablespoons (1 stick) softened butter
2 tablespoons minced fresh tarragon

Lemon-Dill Butter

8 tablespoons (1 stick) softened butter
3 tablespoons chopped fresh dill
½ teaspoon lemon juice
1 teaspoon Dijon-style mustard

Basil-Garlic Butter

8 tablespoons (1 stick) softened butter
¼ cup chopped fresh basil leaves
1 clove garlic, minced

Chive-Mustard Butter

8 tablespoons (1 stick) softened butter
3 tablespoons chopped fresh chives
1 teaspoon Dijon-style mustard

Remove giblets and reserve for use another time. Split hens lengthwise, rinse, and pat dry. Season with salt and pepper and set aside.

Preheat grill and lightly coat with oil or cooking spray. Prepare herb butter of choice by combining ingredients until well blended. Cover and refrigerate until ready to use.

When grill is ready, place hens on prepared grill, skin-side up, 4 to 6 inches from source of heat. Spread herb butter generously over skin. Grill 7 to 8 minutes and turn hens over. Spread with herb butter and grill 7 to 8 minutes. Repeat, turning hens 2 more times, spreading with herb butter each time. Cook about 30 minutes or until temperature on meat thermometer is 170°F and juices run clear when thighs are pierced with fork.

6 to 8 servings

Notes: Add hickory or mesquite wood chips to fire when grilling to add a different flavor. Hens may also be cooked in broiler. Make extra herb butter to spread on corn-on-the-cob.

Cornish Hens with Bama Barbecue Sauce

INGREDIENTS

4 *Gold Kist Farms* Cornish Hens
(1 pound 6 ounces each)
Salt and freshly ground pepper to taste

SAUCE

⅔ cup orange marmalade
⅓ cup steak sauce or barbecue sauce
¼ cup Worcestershire sauce
¼ cup lemon juice

Variation: Preheat oven to 400° F. Place hens on rack in roasting pan, cover, and bake 25 minutes. Remove from oven and discard drippings. Reduce oven temperature to 350° F. Dip hens in sauce as above and bake, uncovered, 20 to 30 minutes or until hens test done as in recipe.

Remove giblets and reserve for use another time. Split hens lengthwise, rinse, and pat dry. Season with salt and pepper.

Place hens in circle in large microproof dish with thickest portion at outer edge of dish. Cover and microcook on HIGH 20 to 25 minutes.

Place sauce ingredients in 2-cup measuring cup and beat with whisk until well combined. Pour into pie place and set aside.

Preheat grill and lightly coat with oil or cooking spray.

Remove hens from microwave oven and dip in reserved sauce to coat on all sides. When grill is ready, place hens, skin-side up, on prepared grill 4 to 6 inches from source of heat. Cook 15 to 20 minutes, turning frequently, until temperature on meat thermometer is 170° F and juices run clear when thighs are pierced with fork.

6 to 8 servings

Cornish Hens with Bama
Barbecue Sauce, facing page

Grecian Chicken Breasts, page 125

ENTERTAINING

Parisian Walnut-Dijon Chicken

INGREDIENTS

- 6 *Gold Kist Farms* boneless, skinless, split chicken breasts
- 1 tablespoon butter or margarine
- ½ cup minced onion
- 1 clove garlic, minced
- ¼ cup (2 ounces) cream cheese
- ¾ cup finely chopped walnuts
- Salt and freshly ground pepper to taste
- 4 tablespoons Dijon-style mustard, divided
- ½ cup half and half
- ½ cup peeled and seeded chopped tomatoes
- 2 tablespoons chopped fresh parsley
- 1 small onion, sliced and sautéed to garnish (optional)
- Hot cooked rice or pasta to serve (optional)

Place chicken breasts between sheets of plastic wrap and pound with meat mallet to ¼-inch thickness. Set aside.

Melt butter in small skillet. Add minced onion and cook 3 minutes. Add garlic and cook 1 to 2 minutes or until onion is transparent. Stir in cream cheese, walnuts, salt, and pepper. Cook about 1 minute, stirring. Set aside.

Preheat broiler. Lightly grease baking sheet or shallow baking dish and set aside.

Remove half of walnut mixture, reserving half for sauce. Place breasts flat on work surface and spoon about 1 tablespoon walnut mixture near edge on left side of each breast. Fold right sides over filling and secure edges with wooden toothpicks. Place on prepared baking sheet. Set 1 tablespoon mustard aside. Brush remaining 3 tablespoons mustard on both sides of chicken. Broil 4 to 6 inches from source of heat 6 to 8 minutes on each side or until no longer pink inside.

To make sauce, place reserved walnut mixture, remaining tablespoon mustard, half and half, tomatoes, and parsley in saucepan. Simmer over low heat, stirring, until slightly thickened, about 2 to 3 minutes.

To serve, remove and discard toothpicks from chicken. Place chicken on serving platter and spoon sauce over. Garnish with sautéed onions and serve with rice or pasta, if desired.

6 servings.

Chicken-Crab Meat Charles

INGREDIENTS

4 *Gold Kist Farms* boneless, skinless, split chicken breasts
Juice and grated zest of 1 lime
1 teaspoon dried thyme leaves
Salt and white pepper to taste
4 tablespoons (½ stick) unsalted butter or margarine, divided
2 tablespoons minced onion
1 can (8 ounces) crab meat, drained and picked over
1 cup cooked hollandaise sauce

Place chicken breasts between sheets of plastic wrap and pound with meat mallet to ¼-inch thickness. Place lime juice in small bowl (reserve zest for later use), and stir in thyme, salt, and pepper. Brush breasts on both sides and set aside.

Melt 1 tablespoon butter in small skillet, add onion, and cook until onion is transparent. Stir in crab meat and cook, stirring gently, until heated through. Remove from heat, set aside, and keep warm.

Melt remaining 3 tablespoons butter in large skillet. Add chicken breasts and sauté 4 to 5 minutes on each side until browned and no longer pink inside. Remove to serving platter or individual dishes.

Stir reserved lime zest into hollandaise sauce. Spoon ¼ of crab mixture on each breast and top with dollop of hollandaise sauce. Pass remaining sauce separately. Serve immediately.

4 servings

Chicken Kiev

INGREDIENTS

- ½ cup (1 stick) butter, softened (no substitution)
- 2 tablespoons snipped chives
- 2 tablespoons chopped fresh parsley
- 6 *Gold Kist Farms* boneless, skinless, split chicken breasts
- 2 eggs, lightly beaten
- 1 cup fine dry bread crumbs
- Salt and freshly ground pepper to taste
- Vegetable oil for cooking

Place butter, chives, and parsley in bowl and mix with fork or wooden spoon until well combined. Shape into 3-inch long roll and wrap in plastic wrap. Place in freezer until very firm.

Place chicken breasts between sheets of plastic wrap and pound with meat mallet to ¼-inch thickness. Remove butter from freezer and cut into six ½-inch cubes. Place 1 cube in center of each breast. Fold sides over and roll up, enclosing butter completely. Secure with wooden toothpicks. Place beaten eggs in shallow dish. Place bread crumbs, seasoned with salt and pepper, in separate shallow dish. Dip rolls in beaten eggs and roll in seasoned bread crumbs. Place on plate, cover, and refrigerate at least 1 hour.

Heat 2 to 3 inches oil in deep-fat fryer or large heavy saucepan. Use slotted spoon to lower 3 rolls into hot oil. Deep-fry about 15 minutes or until rolls are golden brown.

Remove with slotted spoon and drain on paper towels. Keep warm while cooking remaining rolls. Remove toothpicks before serving. Serve immediately.

6 servings

Inside-Out Chicken Cordon Bleu

INGREDIENTS

- 4 *Gold Kist Farms* boneless, skinless, split chicken breasts
- 4 slices (about ¼ pound) Monterey Jack or Swiss cheese
- About ½ pound thinly sliced prosciutto or ham (see Note)
- 4 tablespoons (½ stick) butter or margarine, divided
- ¼ pound fresh mushrooms, sliced
- 1 tablespoon olive or vegetable oil
- ¼ teaspoon dried sage
- Salt and freshly ground pepper to taste
- 1 cup heavy cream

Note: Prosciutto is available at Italian delicatessen or in delicatessen section of supermarket.

Place chicken breasts between sheets of plastic wrap and pound with meat mallet to ¼-inch thickness. Place 1 slice cheese on top of each chicken breast and roll up, enclosing filling completely. Wrap with prosciutto and secure with wooden toothpicks. Set aside.

Melt 2 tablespoons butter in medium-size skillet and sauté mushrooms until limp. Remove with slotted spoon and set aside. Melt remaining 2 tablespoons butter with 1 tablespoon oil in skillet. Stir in sage, salt, and pepper. Add rolled chicken breasts and cook about 5 minutes on each side until prosciutto begins to brown and is crusty. Reduce heat and add cream slowly. Do not allow to boil. Stir in reserved mushrooms and simmer 3 to 5 minutes until cream begins to thicken and chicken is no longer pink inside. Remove and discard toothpicks and serve immediately.

4 servings

Smoky Sesame Chicken Rolls

INGREDIENTS

4 *Gold Kist Farms* boneless, skinless, split chicken breasts
1 tablespoon sesame oil
1 tablespoon finely chopped fresh thyme or 1 teaspoon dried thyme
Salt and freshly ground pepper to taste
½ cup (2 ounces) shredded smoked cheese, Gouda suggested
½ cup fine dry bread crumbs
3 tablespoons sesame seed
1 egg, beaten
Vegetable oil for cooking

SAUCE

1 tablespoon butter or margarine
1 tablespoon sesame oil
2 tablespoons all-purpose flour
¾ cup chicken broth
¼ cup light cream or half and half
¼ cup (1 ounce) shredded smoked cheese, Gouda suggested

Place chicken breasts between 2 sheets of plastic wrap and pound with meat mallet to ¼-inch thickness. Sprinkle breasts evenly with sesame oil and season with thyme, salt, and pepper. Top each breast with ⅛ cup cheese. Fold sides over and roll up, enclosing filling completely. Secure with wooden toothpicks.

Place bread crumbs on plate and stir in sesame seed. Dip each breast in beaten egg and roll in bread crumb mixture to coat.

Heat 2 to 3 inches oil in deep-fat fryer or large heavy saucepan. Use slotted spoon to lower rolls into hot oil. Deep-fry about 15 minutes or until rolls are golden brown. Remove with slotted spoon and drain on paper towels. Keep warm while preparing sauce.

Place butter and sesame oil in medium-size saucepan. When butter has melted add flour and stir until smooth. Add chicken broth and cream slowly off heat, stirring constantly. Return to low heat and stir until thickened. Stir in cheese and cook until cheese has melted.

To serve, remove toothpicks from chicken rolls and place rolls on serving plate or individual dishes. Spoon sauce over.

4 servings

Basil-Crusted Chicken Oriental

INGREDIENTS

- 6 *Gold Kist Farms* boneless, skinless, split chicken breasts
- 4 tablespoons (½ stick) butter or margarine, melted
- 2 tablespoons Hoisin sauce (see Note)
- 1 tablespoon plus 1 teaspoon Chinese-style mustard
- ⅔ cup Panko Japanese-style bread crumbs (see Note), or plain dry bread crumbs
- 3 tablespoons chopped fresh basil or 1 tablespoon dried basil (fresh preferred)
- 2 tablespoons grated Parmesan cheese

SAUCE

- ½ cup light or regular dairy sour cream
- 2 tablespoons tomato paste or Hoisin sauce
- 2 teaspoons Chinese-style mustard
- 1 teaspoon light or regular soy sauce
- 1 small plum tomato, peeled and diced

❖ ❖ ❖ ❖

- 1 small plum tomato, peeled and diced to garnish
- Fresh basil leaves to garnish (optional)

Note: Hoisin sauce and Panko Japanese-style bread crumbs are available in Asian food section of the supermarket.

Preheat oven to 500° F. Lightly grease 1 large or 2 small baking pans and set aside. Rinse chicken breasts and pat dry. Set aside.

Place butter, Hoisin sauce, and mustard in shallow dish and mix well. Mix bread crumbs, basil, and cheese in separate shallow dish. Dip breasts in butter mixture, then in bread crumb mixture, coating well on all sides. Place in single layer in prepared baking pan(s).

Bake in preheated oven, uncovered, 8 minutes. Reduce heat to 450° F and bake 7 minutes or until crumb coating is golden brown and chicken is no longer pink inside.

To prepare sauce, place sour cream, tomato paste, mustard, and soy sauce in microproof bowl or saucepan and stir to blend. Stir in 1 diced tomato. Cover and heat in microwave oven on HIGH 30 seconds, or heat in saucepan just until warmed.

To serve, spoon sauce onto warmed serving platter. Arrange breasts on sauce, or cut breasts crosswise into thick slices and arrange over sauce. Sprinkle chicken with remaining diced tomato and garnish with basil, if desired.

6 servings

Pesto and Pepper Chicken Rolls

INGREDIENTS

- 6 *Gold Kist Farms* boneless, skinless, split chicken breasts
- 7½ ounces (half of 15-ounce jar) pesto, or more to taste
- 2 cups (8 ounces) shredded Monterey Jack cheese
- 1 jar (16 ounces) roasted red bell peppers, drained
- 2 tablespoons peppercorns, crushed

Preheat oven to 350° F. Lightly coat baking pan with oil or cooking spray and set aside.

Place chicken breasts between sheets of plastic wrap and pound with meat mallet to ¼-inch thickness. Spread generous layer of pesto over each breast and sprinkle with cheese. Top with whole pieces of roasted pepper and roll up breasts jelly-roll style. Secure with wooden toothpicks. Press crushed peppercorns evenly into chicken rolls.

Place rolls in prepared pan and bake in preheated oven 45 minutes or until chicken is no longer pink inside. Remove and discard toothpicks and serve immediately.

6 servings

▲ Pesto and Pepper Chicken Roll, facing page

▼ Chicken Boursin en Croûte, page 124

Chicken Boursin en Croûte

INGREDIENTS

- 4 *Gold Kist Farms* boneless, skinless, split chicken breasts
- 1 package (5 ounces) pepper-spiced Boursin cheese, softened
- 1 tablespoon fresh thyme or 1 teaspoon dried thyme
- 8 large shrimp, peeled, deveined, cooked, and cut in half lengthwise
- 1 cup chicken broth
- 8 phyllo leaves (approximately 1/3 of 16-ounce box), thawed if frozen
- Melted butter for brushing (no substitution)

SAUCE

- 2 shallots, minced
- 3/4 cup chicken broth
- 1 cup Madeira
- 1 tablespoon honey
- 1 tablespoon coarse-grain mustard
- 1 tablespoon butter or margarine

Place chicken breasts between sheets of plastic wrap and pound with meat mallet to 1/4-inch thickness. Cut cheese into 4 equal-size pieces and place 1 piece on each breast. Spread cheese on breasts to within 1/2 inch of edges on all sides. Sprinkle thyme on breasts and top each breast with 4 shrimp halves. Fold sides over and roll up to enclose filling completely. Secure with wooden toothpicks.

Place rolls, seam-side down, in 10-inch skillet. Add 1 cup chicken broth, cover, and cook on medium heat 5 to 7 minutes. Remove with slotted spoon and place on rack or paper towels to drain. Reserve liquid in skillet for sauce.

Preheat oven to 375°F. Lightly grease baking sheet and set aside.

Remove 8 phyllo leaves from package and unfold on flat dry surface. Cover with damp kitchen towel. Remove 1 leaf and place on work surface. Brush with melted butter. Cover with second leaf and brush with butter. Place 1 chicken roll lengthwise on leaves 2 inches in from short end. Fold bottom edge of leaves up over chicken, then fold long sides over. Brush top of covered roll with butter and roll over once toward top of leaf. Brush with butter, roll again, brushing and rolling to top of leaf. Repeat with remaining 3 chicken rolls.

Place on prepared baking sheet, seam-side down. Bake in preheated oven 15 to 20 minutes or until golden brown.

To make sauce, bring reserved liquid to a boil. Add shallots and cook 3 minutes. Stir in 3/4 cup chicken broth and Madeira. Cook, uncovered, over high heat until reduced by almost half. Stir in honey, mustard, and butter. Cook 2 minutes. Place chicken rolls on platter and place sauce in small bowl to pass separately.

4 servings

Grecian Chicken Breasts

INGREDIENTS

- 6 *Gold Kist Farms* boneless, skinless, split chicken breasts
- Salt and freshly ground pepper to taste
- 1 package (10 ounces) frozen chopped spinach, thawed
- 8 ounces feta cheese, crumbled
- ½ cup mayonnaise
- 1 clove garlic, minced
- ¼ cup all-purpose flour
- ½ teaspoon paprika
- 12 strips bacon

Note: This dish can be prepared ahead of time, covered, and refrigerated or wrapped and frozen until ready to bake. If frozen, thaw in refrigerator before baking.

Preheat oven to 325°F.

Cut pocket in chicken breasts and season inside pocket and surface of chicken with salt and pepper. Set aside.

Squeeze liquid from thawed spinach and place, uncooked, in bowl. Add cheese, mayonnaise, and garlic and stir to combine. Spoon into pockets in chicken, dividing evenly.

Place flour on plate and stir in paprika. Lightly coat stuffed chicken breasts. Wrap 2 strips bacon around each breast and secure with wooden toothpicks. Place on rack in baking pan and bake, uncovered, in preheated oven 1 hour or until chicken is no longer pink inside. Remove toothpicks before serving.

6 servings

Blue Bayou Chicken Breasts

INGREDIENTS

6 *Gold Kist Farms* boneless, split chicken breasts with skin attached
6 tablespoons (3/4 stick) butter or margarine, divided
2 medium-size onions, chopped
5 scallions (green onions), thinly sliced
2 cloves garlic, minced
12 ounces fresh mushrooms, chopped
6 ounces bleu cheese, crumbled
1 cup fresh bread crumbs
1 package (16 ounces) hot, cooked linguine
1 package (10 ounces) frozen chopped spinach, thawed and squeezed dry
2 tablespoons minced fresh parsley
Parsley sprigs and sliced tomatoes or tomato roses to garnish

Variation: Boneless thighs with skin can be substituted for chicken breasts.

Preheat oven to 350° F. Lightly grease large shallow baking pan and set aside. Rinse chicken and pat dry. Loosen skin from flesh, leaving skin attached to breasts on 1 side. Set aside.

Melt 2 tablespoons butter in large skillet and cook onions until transparent. Add scallions and garlic and cook just until onions are lightly browned. Spoon into large bowl using slotted spoon. Add mushrooms to drippings in skillet and sauté, stirring often, until most of liquid has evaporated. Add to onion mixture and stir in bleu cheese and bread crumbs. Mix well.

Spoon cheese mixture between skin and flesh of each chicken breast. Tuck edges of skin under breast and secure with wooden toothpicks. Place breasts, skin-side up, in prepared baking pan. Melt remaining 4 tablespoons butter and brush on each breast. Bake, uncovered, in preheated oven 40 to 50 minutes or until no longer pink inside, basting occasionally with pan juices. Remove breasts from baking pan and remove and discard toothpicks. Set aside and keep warm.

Add hot linguine and spinach to drippings in baking pan and toss gently to mix and coat with drippings. Spread mixture on serving platter and arrange chicken breasts on top. Sprinkle chicken with minced parsley and garnish with parsley sprigs and tomatoes.

6 servings

Chicken for a Crowd

INGREDIENTS

16 to 18 *Gold Kist Farms* boneless, skinless chicken thighs (about 4 pounds)
Salt and freshly ground pepper to taste
1 large onion, chopped
1 can (6 ounces) orange juice concentrate, undiluted
½ cup orange marmalade
2 tablespoons Worcestershire sauce
Grated zest from 1 orange
½ teaspoon white pepper
½ cup sliced almonds
Dark raisins, orange slices, and parsley to garnish
Hot, cooked rice to serve

Preheat oven to 375°F.

Rinse chicken and pat dry. Place in 12 × 9 × 2-inch baking dish. Season with salt and pepper and sprinkle with chopped onion. Place orange juice concentrate, marmalade, Worcestershire, zest, and white pepper in small bowl. Stir to combine and pour over chicken.

Bake, uncovered, in preheated oven 30 minutes, basting frequently with sauce. Turn chicken and cook, basting frequently, 20 to 30 minutes or until chicken is opaque. Add almond slices during last 10 minutes of cooking.

To serve, spoon rice into serving dish and arrange chicken over rice. Spoon sauce in baking dish over chicken and garnish with raisins, orange slices, and parsley.

8 to 10 servings

Tangy Cornish Hens

INGREDIENTS

- 4 *Gold Kist Farms* Cornish Hens (1 pound 6 ounces each)
- Salt and freshly ground pepper to taste
- 4 tablespoons (½ stick) butter or margarine
- 1 jar (10½ ounces) red pepper jelly
- 2 tablespoons cider vinegar

Preheat oven to 350° F. Lightly grease large baking pan and set aside.

Remove giblets and set aside for use another time. Split hens lengthwise, rinse, and pat dry. Season on both sides with salt and pepper and place in single layer, skin-side up, in prepared pan.

Melt butter in saucepan. Stir in jelly and vinegar and cook just until jelly has melted. Stir to blend. Brush hens with jelly glaze and roast in preheated oven 35 to 40 minutes, basting with remaining glaze every 15 minutes. Cook until temperature on meat thermometer is 170° F and juices run clear when thighs are pierced with fork.

6 to 8 serving

Tangy Cornish Hens,
facing page

Cornish Hens with Barley Dressing

INGREDIENTS

- 4 *Gold Kist Farms* Cornish Hens (1 pound 6 ounces each)
- Salt and freshly ground pepper to taste

DRESSING

- 4 tablespoons (½ stick) butter or margarine
- 1 cup quick-cooking fine pearl barley
- 1 onion, chopped
- 1 stalk celery, sliced
- 1½ cups chicken broth
- 1 package (2 ounces) dehydrated onion soup mix
- ½ cup slivered almonds

SAUCE

- 2 tablespoons olive oil
- 2 tablespoons butter or margarine
- 2 cups sliced fresh mushrooms
- 1 clove garlic, minced
- 2 tablespoons all-purpose flour
- 1½ cups chicken broth
- 3 tablespoons dry red wine
- 2 tablespoons minced parsley

Preheat oven to 350° F. Lightly grease 2-quart casserole and set aside.

Remove giblets and set aside for use another time. Rinse hens, pat dry, and season inside and out with salt and pepper.

Tie legs together and place hens, breast-side up, on rack in baking pan. Roast 1 hour or until temperature on meat thermometer is 180° F and juices run clear when thighs are pierced with fork.

To make dressing, melt 4 tablespoons butter in skillet. Add barley, onion, and celery. Cook 4 to 5 minutes or until barley is golden and vegetables are tender. Stir in 1½ cups broth, onion soup mix, and almonds. Pour into prepared casserole, cover, and bake in preheated oven 1 hour.

To make sauce, heat olive oil and 2 tablespoons butter in saucepan. Add mushrooms and cook about 3 minutes until almost softened. Add garlic and cook 2 minutes. Stir in flour and cook, stirring, 2 minutes. Pour 1½ cups broth into saucepan slowly, stirring constantly, until thickened. Stir in wine and parsley.

To serve, place hens on serving platter and surround with barley dressing. Spoon sauce over or serve separately.

4 to 6 servings

Cornish Hens with Barley Dressing,
facing page

Mustard Glazed Cornish Hens

INGREDIENTS

- 6 *Gold Kist Farms* Cornish Hens (1 pound 6 ounces each)
- ¾ cup Dijon-style mustard
- 2 tablespoons chopped fresh rosemary or 2 teaspoons dried rosemary
- 1 clove garlic, minced
- 1 tablespoon soy sauce
- 6 tablespoons extra virgin olive oil

Preheat oven to 350° F.

Remove giblets and set aside for use another time. Split hens lengthwise, rinse, pat dry, and remove skin. Place in single layer, breast-side down, on rack in shallow roasting pan. Set aside.

Place mustard in 2-cup measuring cup and stir in rosemary, garlic, and soy sauce. Add oil very slowly, beating constantly with whisk.

Coat hens with mustard mixture, turn breast-side up, and brush on second side. Roast in preheated oven 35 to 40 minutes, basting occasionally, until temperature on meat thermometer is 170° F and juices run clear when thighs are pierced with fork.

Place on platter to serve.

10 to 12 servings

Cornish Hens with Oyster-Corn Bread Stuffing

INGREDIENTS

- 6 *Gold Kist Farms* Cornish Hens (1 pound 6 ounces each)
- ½ pint (about 12) medium-size shucked oysters
- 3 cups crumbled corn bread
- 1½ cups cubed white bread
- ¾ cup chopped onion
- ½ cup chopped celery
- 1 egg, well beaten
- 1 cup chicken broth
- ½ teaspoon poultry seasoning
- Salt and freshly ground pepper to taste
- ½ cup (or more as needed) melted butter or margarine for basting
- Paprika (optional)

Note: For moister stuffing, add additional chicken broth or pan drippings to stuffing mixture. Paprika, sprinkled over surface of hens before roasting, will add golden brown color to cooked hens.

Remove giblets and set aside for use another time. Rinse hens, pat dry, and set aside.

Rinse and drain oysters, cut into quarters, and place in large bowl. Add corn bread, white bread cubes, onion, celery, egg, chicken broth, poultry seasoning, salt, and pepper. Mix with large spoon or hands until well combined. Spoon about ½ cup stuffing into each hen cavity.

Preheat oven to 350°F.

Truss cavities to close, fold wing tips back under upper part of wings, and tie legs together. Brush entire surface of hens with melted butter and sprinkle with paprika, if desired.

Place, breast-side up, on rack in large roasting pan. Roast in preheated oven 1 hour 30 minutes, basting occasionally, until temperature on meat thermometer is 180°F, center of stuffing is 165°F, and juices run clear when thighs are pierced with fork.

6 servings

Variation: Stuffing may be baked separately in covered casserole. Bake about 30 minutes. Uncover during last 5 minutes of baking if crisp top is desired. If hens are roasted unstuffed, reduce cooking time by about 15 minutes.

Cornish Hens with Lemon & Black Bean-Rice

INGREDIENTS

- 4 *Gold Kist Farms* Cornish Hens (1 pound 6 ounces each)
- 1 lemon, thinly sliced
- 2 tablespoons olive oil

RICE

- 1 cup rice
- 1¾ cups chicken broth
- Juice of 2 lemons
- 1 teaspoon grated lemon zest
- 2 stalks celery, sliced
- 1 onion, chopped
- 1 tablespoon butter or margarine
- ½ teaspoon ground coriander
- Pinch of sugar
- ½ cup cooked black beans, drained and rinsed
- ¼ cup toasted slivered almonds

SAUCE

- 2 tablespoons cornstarch
- 2 tablespoons light brown sugar
- ½ teaspoon paprika
- Salt and freshly ground pepper to taste
- ½ cup chicken broth

Note: Cornish Hens may be split in half lengthwise before serving if smaller portions are desired.

Preheat oven to 400°F. Remove giblets and set aside for use another time.

Rinse hens and pat dry. Lift skin over breast and place 2 or 3 lemon slices between meat and skin on each hen. Rub entire surface of hens with oil. Tie legs together and place hens, breast-side up, on rack in roasting pan. Reduce oven temperature to 350°F and roast 1 hour, basting occasionally, or until temperature on meat thermometer is 180°F and juices run clear when thighs are pierced with fork.

To prepare rice, place rice, broth, lemon juice, lemon zest, celery, onion, butter, coriander, and sugar in saucepan. Cover and simmer 20 minutes or until rice is done. Stir in black beans and almonds. Keep warm until ready to serve.

To make sauce, place cornstarch, brown sugar, paprika, salt, and pepper in small bowl and stir to combine. Pour broth into bowl slowly, stirring to blend. When hens are done, set aside and keep warm. Remove rack from roasting pan and place pan on cooktop over low heat. Pour sauce into pan, stirring to deglaze pan. Keep warm.

To serve, spoon rice mixture onto serving platter and arrange hens over rice. Drizzle sauce over hens.

4 to 6 servings

Cornish Hens with Lemon and Black Bean Rice, facing page

Lloyd Sumner farm, Ellijay, GA

Chicken Basics

Chicken Basics

Chickens were introduced to the New World in the 1500s by Spanish explorers. Today, chicken is America's number one meat choice. The average American eats about 74 pounds a year. Why chicken? Taste is the main reason, followed by nutritional benefits, versatility, low fat content, convenience, and value. Chicken also fits perfectly into today's hectic lifestyles. Boneless, skinless chicken breast, the most versatile and fastest cooking cut of chicken, is served more often than any other cut by almost half of those who buy chicken.

There are literally thousands of ways to prepare chicken. But, there's more to chicken than just recipes. Take time to look over Chicken Basics. The information you find will provide you with useful tips on how to select, store, prepare, and cook chicken, as well as important safety guidelines. Together, they will ensure your ability to cook delicious, safe meals from the recipes in this book and all of your long-time favorite recipes as well.

BUYING CHICKEN

LOOK FOR FRESHNESS

After selecting a recipe from *Simply the Best Chicken*, it's time to go shopping. This is when the safe handling of chicken begins. Follow the tips below to select the freshest possible chicken.

- Buy chicken at the end of a shopping trip to minimize time out of refrigeration.
- Meat should be firm but yield to touch. You can test this by pressing your fingertip into the flesh.
- Overall skin color can range from deep yellow to white, but should not be blotchy. Color is not an indicator of nutritional value, flavor, tenderness, or fat content. It's a result of the chicken's diet.
- Check the "sell by" date printed on the label. With proper handling, chicken will remain fresh up to 3 days beyond the "sell by" date. But, just to be safe, cook or freeze chicken as soon as possible after purchase.

LOOK FOR QUALITY

Extensive measures are taken to ensure that all *Gold Kist Farms* chickens shipped to market are safe and wholesome. Government inspectors inspect chickens to be sure they meet United States Department of Agriculture standards for Grade A and, in addition, *Gold Kist* inspectors inspect every chicken to be sure that it exceeds government standards.

WHOLESOMENESS

When you see a USDA inspection stamp on chicken, it means the chicken has undergone the USDA Food Safety and Inspection Service mandatory inspection. This inspection ensures chicken is wholesome, properly labeled, and not adulterated. It also means that the processing plant and its equipment and procedures have passed inspection.

LABELING FOR SAFETY

USDA requires that instructions for safe handling and cooking appear on all packages of raw poultry. Poultry inspection procedures are designed to minimize the presence of harmful bacteria in poultry. However, even with careful inspection, some bacteria could be present and become a problem if poultry is not handled and prepared properly.

GRADING

Grading involves evaluating poultry in terms of quality standards and degree of excellence. A technically trained government grader awards USDA Grade A only to chickens that meet the highest standard. An official grade shield appears on packages of Grade A chickens to certify this quality standard has been met.

USDA Grade A whole chickens and parts have:

- normal shape and color
- whole bones (not broken or disjointed)
- uniform layer of fat in skin
- no pinfeathers
- no exposed flesh
- no missing parts

USDA Grade A boneless chicken has:

- no bone, cartilage, tendons, bruises, or blood clots

TYPES AND CUTS OF CHICKEN

To meet the needs of today's consumer, chicken is conveniently packaged in a variety of sizes, cuts, quantities, and combinations. Use the chart on page 142 as a guide to buying exactly what you want in appropriate quantities to serve family or guests.

STORING CHICKEN

Chicken, and all fresh meat, is perishable and should be handled and prepared with care to maintain freshness and top quality. Refrigerate or freeze chicken as soon as possible after purchase. Cold temperature helps ensure freshness and keeps bacteria from multiplying. Never leave chicken on the countertop at room temperature.

REFRIGERATING

- Store chicken on a plate to catch any juices that may drip and spread bacteria to other food in the refrigerator. Store on the bottom shelf, the coldest part of the refrigerator.
- Refrigerate at a consistent 40° F or below.
- Raw chicken will keep in the refrigerator up to 2 days if properly handled. Cooked chicken keeps 3 to 4 days (or 1 to 2 days in broth or gravy).

FREEZING

- Divide chicken based on how much you expect to use for a meal and wrap in freezer paper or resealable plastic freezer bags.
- You can also wrap individual pieces of chicken separately in sandwich-size bags and put small bags into a large resealable bag. This enables you to defrost just the amount you need.
- Chicken purchased frozen from the supermarket has been frozen by the producer at its peak freshness. Do not allow it to begin thawing if you intend to keep it frozen.
- Label packages with contents and date of freezing.
- Freeze at a consistent 0° F or below.
- Whole chicken can be frozen up to 1 year, parts up to 9 months, and giblets 3 to 4 months. Cooked parts and cooked chicken dishes can be frozen for 4 months.
- Do not thaw and then refreeze raw or cooked chicken. Quality will be adversely affected.

DEFROSTING

- Defrost chicken in the refrigerator. Estimate 24 hours for a 5-pound roaster and 3 to 9 hours for chicken parts. (Defrosting at room temperature encourages bacteria growth.)
- For quicker defrosting, immerse tightly sealed chicken in cold water. Change water every 20 to 30 minutes to maintain a constant cool temperature. Estimate about 2½ hours for a 5-pound roaster.

TYPES AND CUTS OF CHICKEN

Type or Cut	Description	How Sold	Serving Size (Raw Weight)
broiler or broiler-fryer	• a young, small chicken that weighs between 3 and 4½ lbs. • suitable for any cooking method including roasting, broiling, and grilling	• whole, usually with neck and giblets • whole split (halved) • whole quartered • whole cut up (2 breast halves or split breasts, 2 drumsticks, 2 thighs, 2 wings), may include back and giblets • also sold in parts (see below)	¼ chicken; ¾ to 1 lb. (about 6 to 8 ounces cooked meat per person)
roaster	• a large chicken that weighs between 5 and 8 lbs. • usually roasted whole	• whole with giblets and neck	¾ to 1 lb. (about 6 to 8 ounces cooked meat per person)
Cornish Hen	• a very small hen that usually weighs between 1 and 2 lbs. • cross between White Rock and Cornish chicken	• whole with giblets, sold singly or in packs of 2 to 4 hens • premium size is 22 ounces with giblets	½ to 1 hen
hen, stewing chicken, baking hen	• mature chicken that usually weighs between 4 and 7 lbs. • somewhat tough and stringy in texture, but rich in flavor • requires cooking in liquid (i.e., stewing) to tenderize	• whole, usually frozen	generally used for boned, cooked meat and stock or in stews and simmered dishes
breast	• chest of a chicken • all white meat • meatiest of chicken parts and lowest in calories	• whole • split (halved) • bone-in with and without skin • boneless with and without skin • quarters: half breast, portion of back, with or without wings • boneless tenderloins or tenders (the small solid strip of breast meat attached to underside of boneless breast)	1 split (half) breast bone-in: ¾ to 1 lb. boneless: ⅓ to ⅔ lb.
leg	• includes thigh, or top part of leg, and drumstick, or bottom part of leg • all dark meat	• whole (thighs and drumsticks with no back portion) • drumsticks only • thighs only • boneless, skinless thighs • quarters including drumstick, thigh, and back portion	1 leg, 1 to 2 thighs or drumsticks bone-in: ¾ to 1 lb. boneless: ⅓ to ⅔ lb.
wing	• includes drummette, or meatier top part of wing, mid, flat part of wing, and wing tip • all white meat	• whole • drummettes only • as part of breast quarter • wingettes or mixed segments of wing drummettes and wing mid-joints	4 to 6 whole wings or drummettes: ¾ to 1⅛ lb.
liver	• part of giblets, or chicken organs	• in approximately 1 lb. containers • as part of giblet package	4 to 6 livers: ¼ to ⅓ lb.
gizzard and heart	• part of giblets, or chicken organs	• in approximately 1 lb. packages • as part of giblet package	often used in gravy, stuffing, and stock
back and neck	• bony parts of chicken	• in approximately 1 lb. packages • necks as part of giblet package • backs with quartered chicken	generally used for stock

- To defrost chicken in the microwave oven, follow the manufacturers' instructions (usually defrost button or 30% power). Always cook microwave-defrosted chicken immediately to prevent bacteria growth due to the warm temperature of the chicken.

PREPARING CHICKEN

KEEPING IT SAFE

Today's chicken is safer and more wholesome than ever before. But, no matter how carefully poultry is raised and processed, foodborne illness from salmonella and other bacteria can still come from raw or undercooked poultry, as well as from many other foods. Research has shown that 97% of outbreaks of foodborne illness are the result of improper food handling and preparation. Fortunately, proper handling of chicken prevents foodborne illness.

- Wash work area (cutting board, countertop, sink, plate), utensils, and hands with hot, soapy water before and after handling uncooked chicken.
- Cooked chicken should never be placed on any surface (plate or cutting board) on which raw chicken has been placed unless the plate or cutting board has been thoroughly washed.
- Rinse chicken under cold running water and pat dry with paper towels.
- Do not put raw chicken on the countertop; it may leave bacteria that will contaminate other food.

CUTTING UP AND BONING CHICKEN

It's easy to learn how to cut up and bone chicken, and doing it yourself can save money. To make chicken easy to cut, chill until very cold and, naturally, use your sharpest knife.

Cutting Up Whole Chicken (see illustration page 144)

1. Remove giblet package from cavity.
2. Place chicken on cutting board, breast-side up. Cut skin between thighs and body.
3. Hold 1 leg in each hand, lift chicken and bend legs back until ball of thigh joint pops out of socket.
4. Cut between ball and socket to remove leg with thigh attached. Repeat with other leg.
5. To separate thighs and drumsticks, cut through each leg at joint.
6. Move wing so you can feel joint. Cut between ball and socket. Pull wing away and cut through skin. Repeat with other wing.
7. Turn chicken on its side. To separate breast from back, begin at point where wings were attached and cut where breast joins rib bones. Repeat on other side.
8. For bone-in split chicken breasts, place skin-side down and cut wishbone in half at V of bone. Cut closely down along each side of breast bone.
9. Be sure to save bones, skin, and giblets (except liver) to make stock.

Boning Breasts (see illustration page 145)

1. Hold chicken breast in hands, skin-side down, with pointed end of breast facing out, away from hands. Feel for bone structure at bottom of breast. Starting at the bottom bone, which runs through center of breast, work thumb through the meat to the bone.
2. Continue running thumb between meat and bone working toward the point of the breast. Work closely to the bone, separating meat from center bone and cartilage.
3. When end of cartilage is reached with thumb (at point end of breast), force thumb out, making separation complete.
4. Continue separating and pulling meat from bones, always working with thumb close to bone.
5. Separate meat from rib portion of breast.
6. With bones in one hand and meat portion in the other hand, pull to separate completely. May need to use a knife to free one of the small bones at base of bone structure.

CUTTING UP WHOLE CHICKEN

1. Remove giblet package from cavity.

2. Place chicken on cutting board, breast-side up. Cut skin between thighs and body.

3. Hold 1 leg in each hand, lift chicken and bend legs back until ball of thigh joint pops out of socket.

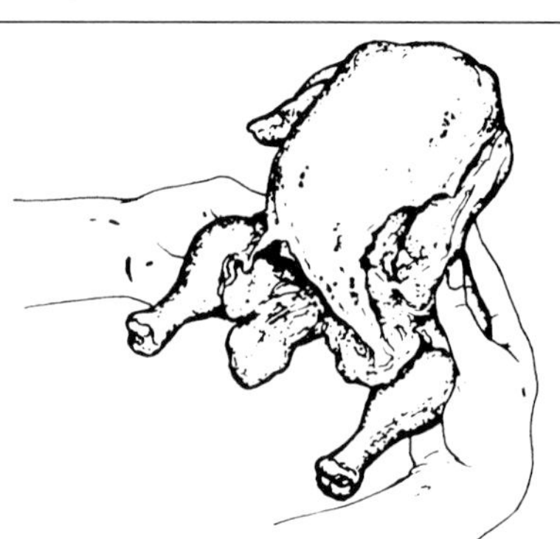

4. Cut between ball and socket to remove leg with thigh attached. Repeat with other leg.

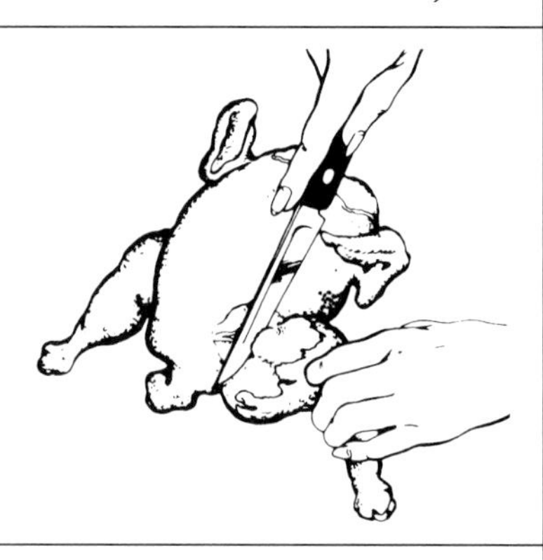

5. To separate thighs and drumsticks, cut through each leg at joint.

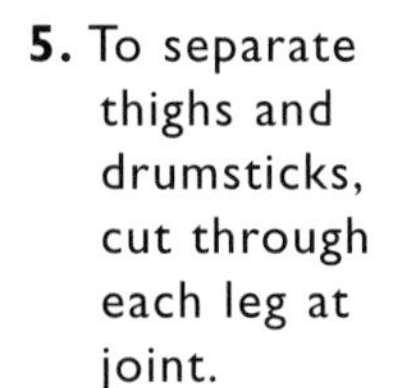

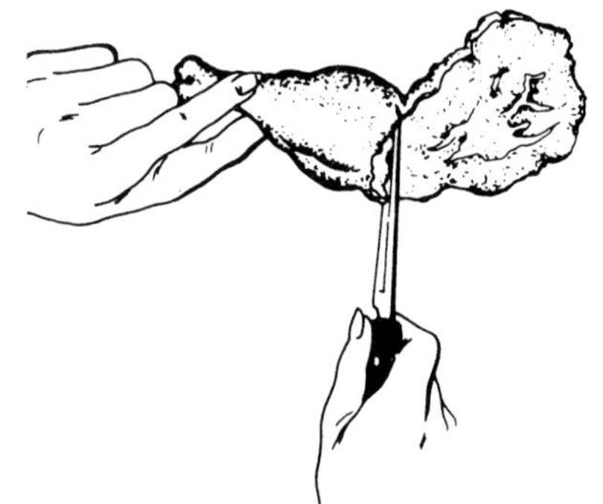

6. Move wing so you can feel joint. Cut between ball and socket. Pull wing away and cut through skin. Repeat with other wing.

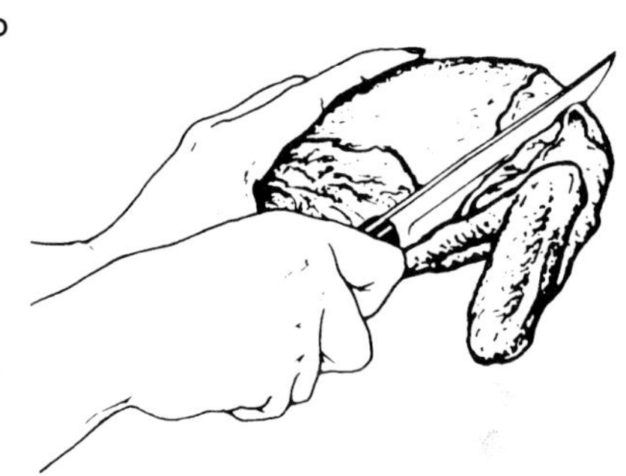

7. Turn chicken on its side. To separate breast from back, begin at point where wings were attached and cut where breast joins rib bones. Repeat on other side.

8. For bone-in split chicken breasts, place skin-side down and cut wishbone in half at V of bone.

Cut closely down along each side of breast bone.

9. Be sure to save bones, skin, and giblets (except liver) to make stock.

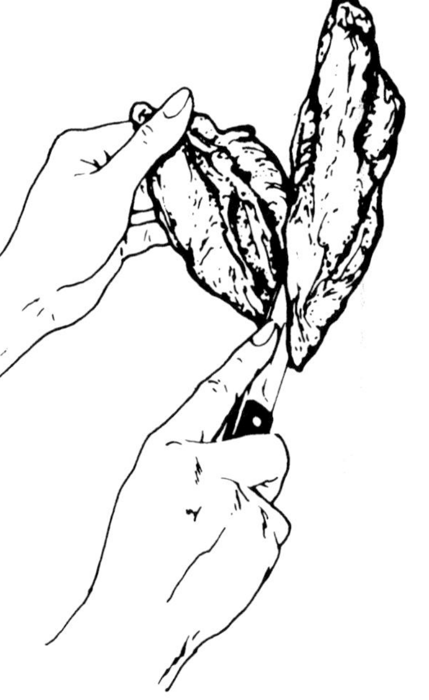

Illustrations courtesy National Broiler Council

BONING BREASTS

1. Hold chicken breast in hands, skin-side down, with pointed end of breast facing out, away from hands. Feel for bone structure at bottom of breast. Starting at the bottom bone, which runs through center of breast, work thumb through the meat to the bone.

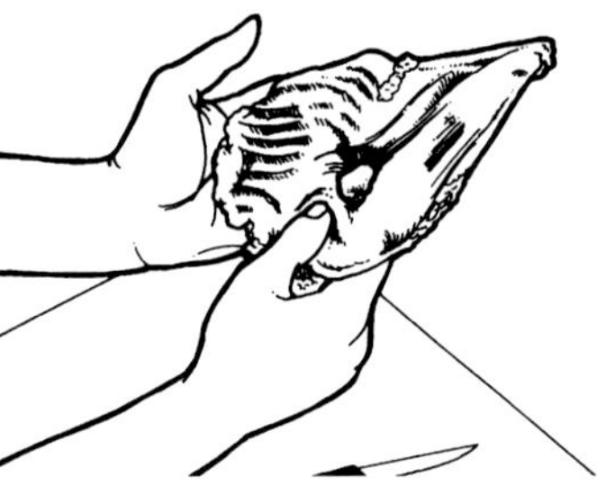

2. Continue running thumb between meat and bone working toward the point of the breast. Work closely to the bone, separating meat from center bone and cartilage.

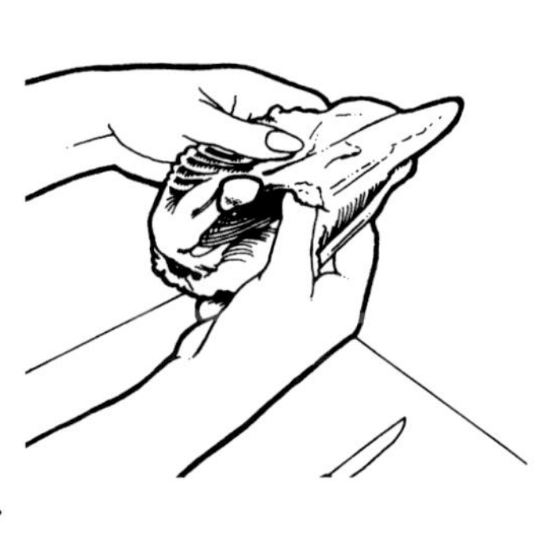

3. When end of cartilage is reached with thumb (at point end of breast), force thumb out, making separation complete.

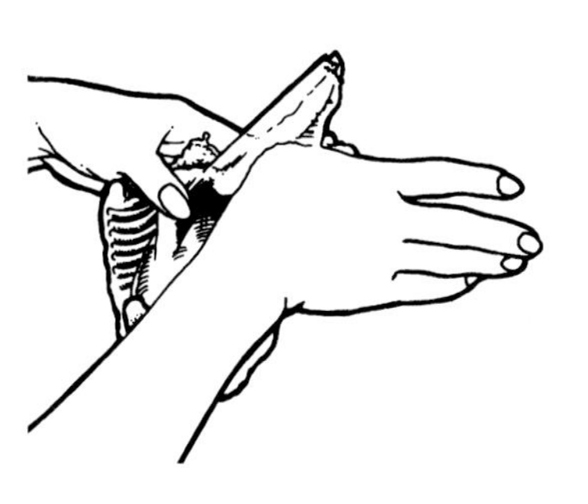

4. Continue separating and pulling meat from bones, always working with thumb close to bone.

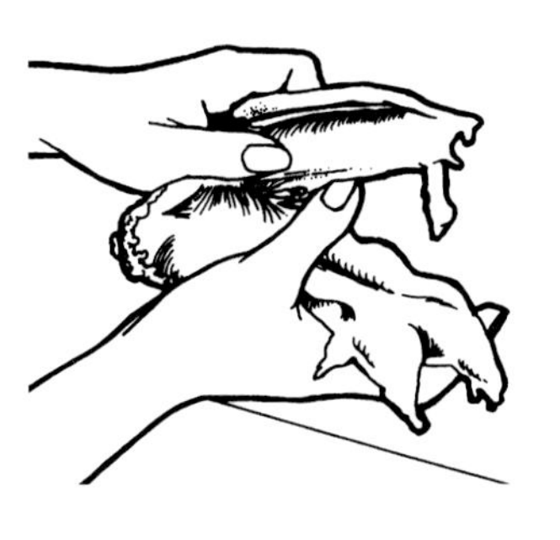

5. Separate meat from rib portion of breast.

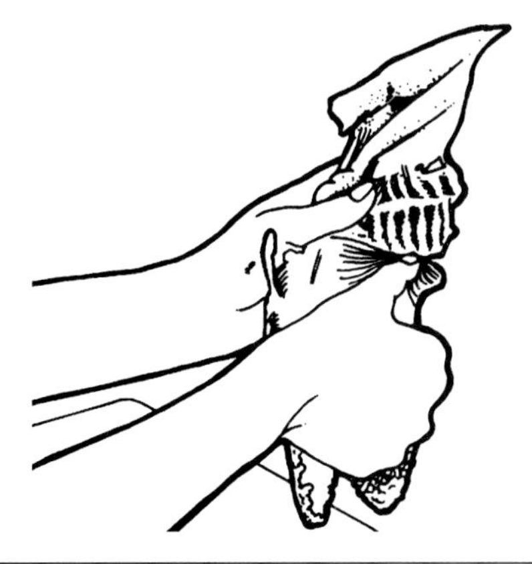

6. With bones in one hand and meat portion in the other hand, pull to separate completely. May need to use a knife to free one of the small bones at base of bone structure.

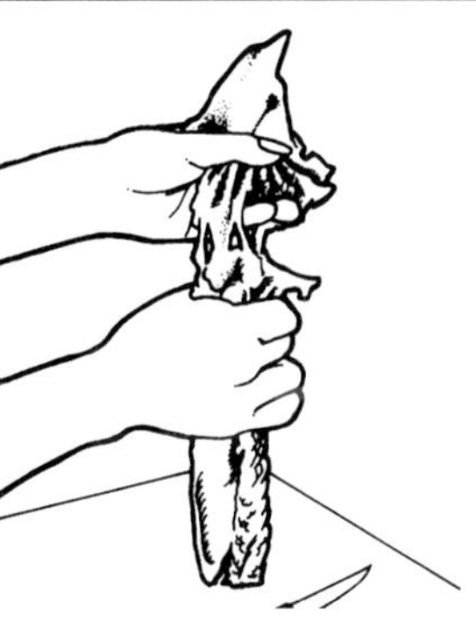

7. Feel to see if a portion of the wishbone (pulley bone) remains. If so, cut away.

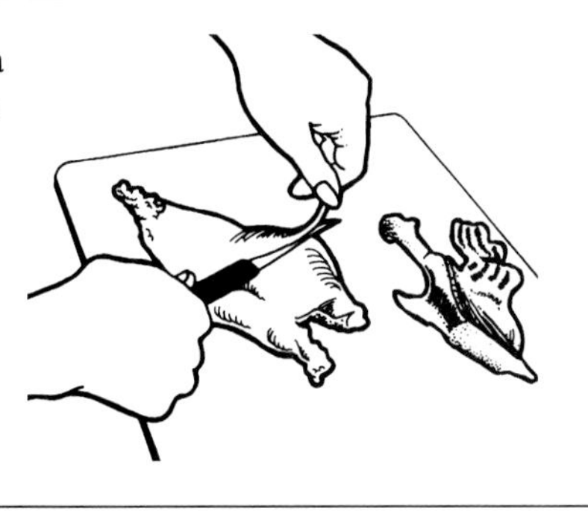

8. If desired, skin may be pulled away and discarded.

without touching the bone.

- Bone-in parts should be cooked to 170° F.
- Boneless parts should be cooked to 160° F.
- Stuffing should be cooked to an internal temperature of 165° F.

Other Tests for Doneness

- Juices should run clear, not pink, when chicken is pierced with a fork.
- Chicken is done when a fork can be inserted with ease, thus the term "fork-tender."
- When cooking a whole bird, the leg should move freely when lifted or twisted.
- When in doubt, remove chicken to a plate and cut with a knife to be sure the meat is opaque and no longer pink in the center or near the bone.

ROASTING AND ROTISSERIE ROASTING

Roasting is the oldest, easiest, and most often used method to cook chicken. To roast is to cook, uncovered, in an oven, allowing the dry heat to circulate completely around the meat. Rotisserie or spit cooking is a variation of roasting in which a spit or rotisserie rod keeps the chicken suspended in the center of the oven or grill, ensuring heat circulation and even cooking and browning.

Conventional Roasting

1. Remove giblets from cavity and remove excess fat. Rinse and pat dry. Season as directed in recipe, or stuff and truss following instructions on page 146.
2. Place, breast-side up, on rack in a shallow, open roasting pan. A rack allows heat to circulate under chicken, providing even cooking and crisp skin on all sides of the chicken.
3. Brush outer surface with oil, butter or margarine, or a combination of both, and sprinkle with salt, if desired. Butter or the addition of paprika aid in browning the skin.
4. Cook, uncovered, in preheated 350° F oven 20 minutes per pound if stuffed, 15 to 17 minutes per pound if unstuffed. Baste with pan drippings, oil, or butter several times during cooking.
5. When done, remove the chicken to carving board, and let stand 15 to 20 minutes before carving to firm the meat and allow juices to retreat back into the meat.

Rotisserie or Spit Roasting

1. Prepare chicken as in Step 1 of "Conventional Roasting." Be sure to truss the chicken to keep its compact shape while turning on the spit.
2. Brush the outer surface with oil, or tie strips of bacon around the chicken when trussing. Then, as the chicken turns, it will baste itself.
3. Follow oven or grill manufacturers' instructions for securing chicken on a spit and operating the rotisserie.
4. When done, turn off heat and allow the chicken to continue turning on spit 15 to 20 minutes before removing. This allows meat to firm and juices to retreat back into the meat.

GRILLING AND BROILING

Grilling and broiling are essentially the same method of cooking with direct, dry heat. The basic difference is whether the source of heat comes from above, in the broiler, or below, on the grill. Both methods cook chicken quickly and seal in its natural juices.

Basting the outside surface of the chicken with oil or a marinade helps seal in juices. They act as a screen to allow heat to penetrate, but prevent natural juices from escaping as steam. If the meat is well basted, steam will be driven back inside the meat, aiding the cooking process and keeping the meat moist and tender.

Chicken may be partially precooked in the microwave oven before it is grilled or broiled to reduce cooking time and maintain juiciness. See "Combination Cooking" on page 151.

Grilling

1. To prevent the chicken from sticking to the grill, lightly coat the grill with oil or cooking spray. Place chicken 4 to 6 inches from the source of heat.
2. If using charcoal, light the coals at least 30 minutes before cooking. They are ready when covered with light gray ash.
3. Place chicken on the grill, skin-side up, with small pieces near the edge of the grill.
4. Turn chicken about every 5 minutes to ensure even cooking and prevent burning. Handle chicken with tongs to keep from puncturing the meat and losing juices.
5. Since many barbecue sauces contain a tomato base or sugar, use only during the last 15 to 20 minutes of grilling to prevent burning.

Broiling

1. Preheat broiler.
2. Season chicken and place, skin-side down, on greased rack in broiler pan. Place 4 to 6 inches from source of heat.
3. Broil until browned, about 15 to 20 minutes on each side.
4. Brush on both sides with marinade, sauce, butter, or oil during broiling.

Combination Cooking — Microcooking and Broiling, Grilling, or Baking

1. Place chicken on a microproof rack or dish with thickest part of chicken at the outer edge of the dish. Cover with wax paper.
2. Microcook chicken three-fourths of time suggested in the manufacturers' manual. Turn chicken over and rotate the dish half-way through cooking.
3. Transfer chicken to the broiler, grill, or oven to finish cooking and crisp skin. Be sure to finish cooking immediately because partially cooked chicken can encourage growth of bacteria.

FRYING

As with roasting, broiling, and grilling, frying is a dry heat method of cooking. The major difference is addition of some form of fat (butter, margarine, or oil). When butter or margarine is used, oil should be added to prevent the butter or margarine from burning. There are several methods of frying.

Sautéing or Pan Frying

To sauté is to cook food quickly in a small amount of fat in a skillet over direct medium-high heat.

1. Rinse chicken and pat dry. Chicken must be very dry to be sautéed successfully.
2. Heat a small amount of fat in a skillet over medium-high heat.
3. Place chicken in the skillet in single layer, skin-side down. If all the pieces of chicken will not fit without overlapping, sauté them in batches.
4. Cook until well browned on both sides.
5. Boneless breasts or thighs are usually done when browned on both sides, but test for doneness to make sure. Larger, bone-in pieces require longer cooking over somewhat reduced heat. Turn frequently during cooking.

Stir-Frying

Stir-frying is a favorite way to cook chicken because it's so quick and easy. You can stir-fry in either a wok or skillet. Use small uniform-size pieces of boneless chicken and other ingredients to ensure even cooking. If you're making a stir-fry dish that includes vegetables, estimate the cooking time for each vegetable and add to the wok, beginning with the vegetable that requires the longest cooking time. For example, broccoli takes longer to cook than pepper strips.

1. Heat the wok or skillet. Add a small amount of oil to the heated utensil.
2. When oil is hot, add chicken and stir constantly until done, adding the remaining ingredients according to the directions in the recipe.

Shallow-Fat Frying and Deep-Frying

To shallow-fry, heat about 2 inches of fat or oil, about enough to half cover food, in a large, heavy skillet and cook over medium heat. To deep-fry, the pan must be deep and there must be enough hot fat to completely cover the meat.

Maintaining a constant correct temperature of the oil is the key to successful frying. If the oil is the right temperature, it will seal the chicken and prevent it from absorbing too much fat. If the oil is too hot, the chicken will dry out and overbrown before it is done. When the oil is not hot enough, the result is greasy chicken. Remember, pieces of white meat cook more quickly than dark meat and small pieces more quickly than large pieces.

1. Season chicken and dip in batter or dredge in flour. Set aside.
2. Heat oil in a skillet or deep-fat fryer until temperature reaches 365°F or a 1-inch cube of bread browns in oil in 1 minute.
3. Use tongs to place the chicken in oil a few pieces at a time. Cook chicken until done, about 10 to 15 minutes on each side to shallow-fry; about 10 to 15 minutes total to deep-fat fry, depending on the size of the chicken pieces.
4. Remove chicken from oil and drain on paper towels. Keep warm.

COOKING WITH MOIST HEAT

Poaching, braising, and stewing are moist-heat cooking methods in which chicken is simmered in wine, water, stock, or a combination of liquids. In smoking, chicken is slowly cooked above, rather than in, a pan of water. Microwave cooking is also a moist-heat cooking method.

Poaching

Poaching is the best way to cook boneless, skinless chicken for use in salads and other dishes that call for cooked chicken. Generally, 1 pound of boneless, skinless chicken yields about 2 to 2½ cups of chopped, cooked chicken.

1. Place chicken in single layer in saucepan and add enough liquid to cover chicken by ½ inch. To enhance flavor, add bay leaf, garlic clove, quartered onion, chunks of carrot and celery, parsley sprigs, peppercorns, or salt, if desired.
2. Bring to a boil, reduce heat, cover, and simmer 12 to 15 minutes.
3. Check for doneness early because over-poaching will toughen chicken.
4. Drain, cool, and refrigerate until ready to use.

Braising and Stewing

Braising and stewing are similar cooking methods. Both are suitable for chicken parts, but are used primarily for large, bone-in pieces such as quarters and for older, larger birds such as stewing or baking hens. Mature birds require a longer cooking time than young birds in order to tenderize the meat. Braising differs from stewing in that chicken is browned in fat before simmering. Braising may be done on top of the stove or in the oven. In both methods, the long, slow cooking develops flavor and tenderizes the meat by breaking down the meat fibers. A tight fitting cover is very important in both methods to prevent liquid from evaporating.

Braising

1. Lightly coat chicken with flour and place in a small amount of hot fat in a large, deep skillet or Dutch oven. Brown about 5 minutes on each side.
2. Discard fat (keep 1 tablespoon for flavor, if desired) and add enough liquid to just cover chicken.
3. Bring to a boil, reduce heat to simmer, cover, and cook several hours or until meat is fork-tender. Add additional liquid during cooking, if necessary.

Stewing

1. Place chicken in large, heavy, deep pot, barely cover

with liquid, and add seasonings.
2. Bring to a boil, reduce heat to simmer, cover, and cook several hours or until meat is fork-tender. Add additional liquid during cooking, if necessary.

Smoking

Smoking is a very slow, easy cooking process that creates a unique flavor in food. Smoked chicken is always moist and tender.

1. Place charcoal pan at the bottom of the smoker to hold both the charcoal and the water-soaked wood chips. When lit, the chips will create smoke that will provide special flavor based on the type of wood burned. (Hickory, pecan, apple, and mesquite are popular woods for smoking.)
2. Heat from the burning charcoal and wood heats the water in the pan placed directly above them, keeping heat low, moist, and even.
3. Place chicken on the grill rack above water pan.
4. Smoke boneless chicken breasts for 30 to 40 minutes, breast quarters 50 to 60 minutes, and whole chickens 4 to 5 hours. The result is worth the wait.

HANDLING CHICKEN AFTER COOKING

Keep these guidelines in mind to keep cooked chicken dishes safe to eat.

- Never leave food at room temperature longer than 2 hours. If cooked chicken is not to be served promptly, it should be kept either hot, between 140° F to 165° F, or cooled and refrigerated at 40° F or less.
- Always reheat leftovers thoroughly before eating. Cover when reheating to retain moisture and guarantee that food will be heated throughout.
- Always store chicken for picnics or lunches in an insulated container or ice chest until ready to eat.
- Cooked, cut up chicken is best when refrigerated no longer than 2 days, whole cooked chicken 3 days.

NUTRITIONAL VALUE

Ounce for ounce, chicken is one of the best sources of low-fat meat protein. It is low in calories, sodium, and cholesterol. Chicken is also a good source of iron and provides significant amounts of key vitamins and minerals including riboflavin, niacin, phosphorus, and potassium.

ONE 3-OUNCE SERVING OF BAKED SKINLESS CHICKEN PROVIDES:

Part	Calories	Protein (grams)	Total Fat (grams)	Saturated Fat (grams)	Cholesterol (milligrams)	Sodium (milligrams)
breast	116	24	2	0	72	63
drumstick	132	23	3	1	79	81
thigh	150	21	7	2	81	75
whole	135	23	4	1	76	73
wing	149	23	6	2	72	78

Source: USDA

Contest Award Winners

A SPECIAL RECOGNITION TO THE FOLLOWING PAST WINNERS OF THE GOLD KIST FARMS® WINNING TASTE RECIPE CONTEST.®

Your interest in foods, love for chicken, and exceptionally creative cooking abilities have enabled us to enjoy these wonderful, delicious recipes. Thank you.

❖ ❖ ❖ ❖

Farah Ahmed Sunnyvale, CA
Tuscan Pesto Chicken Rolls

Sonie J. Alexandre Harvest, AL
Spicy Chinese Chicken Wings

Frances Benthin Scio, OR
Mediterranean Rim Chicken

Gina Bolles Marietta, GA
Tex-Mex Chicken Cups

Gloria Bradley Naperville, IL
Bistro Chicken Sandwiches

Barbara Brenton Naples, FL
Sopa de Pollo y Frijoles (Chicken & Bean Soup)

Alma Carey Sarasota, FL
Chicken Symphonic

Charles E. Davis Naples, FL
Chicken-Crabmeat Charles

Karen Davis Oklahoma City, OK
Peppery Pecan Chicken

Robert "Reid" Decker Andalusia, AL
Chicken Guacamole Salad with Cilantro

Julie DeMatteo Clementon, NJ
Festival Chicken Soup

Dwight Dewsnap Milton, MA
Smoky Sesame Chicken Rolls

Janice Elder Charlotte, NC
Plum Spicy Chicken

Connie Emerson Reno, NV
Chicken Salad with Cajun Dressing

Cynthia E. Evans Sullivan's Island, SC
Greek Marinated Chicken with Feta Cheese

Robyn Feddes Manhattan, MT
Chicken with Apple-Pepper Sauce

Beth Greenfield Evanston, IL
Chicken Fajita Pizza

Eileen Hall Tampa, FL
Grilled Margarita Chicken Sandwiches

Teresa Hannan Smith Sacramento, CA
Basil-Crusted Chicken Oriental

Joni Hilton Cedar Rapids, IA
Pesto and Pepper Chicken Rolls

Carol Hodges Greenacres, FL
Wild & Creamy Chicken-Rice Soup

Betty Hooley Cocoa Beach, FL
Apple Stuffed Chicken Breasts

Kimberly Keough Tampa, FL
Italian Chicken

Liz Klein Fountain Valley, CA
Chicken-Tortellini Salad with Basil Dressing

Nancy Korondon Aurora, IL
Blue Bayou Chicken Breasts

Mary Louise Lever Rome, GA
Mesquite Chicken Burgers with Chutney

Mary Louise Lever Rome, GA
Singapore Chicken Skewers

Dianne C. Mahlert Tallahassee, FL
Chicken Corn-Bread Casserole

Teresa Metzger Louisville, KY
Guadalajara Chicken Olé

Linda Miranda Smithfield, RI
Chicken Lasagna Rolls with Red Pepper Sauce

Manika Misra N. Miami Beach, FL
Parisian Walnut-Dijon Chicken

Linda Morten Katy, TX
Chicken Havana

Susan Muszczynski Chicago, IL
Ricotta Chicken Pie

Gloria B. Norton Jacksonville, FL
Chicken-Broccoli Triangles

Virginia Norton Charlottesville, VA
Hearts of Palm Chicken Salad

Brenda O'Conner Athens, AL
Silky Spicy Chicken

Marjorie Ohrenstein Los Angeles, CA
Spicy Potato Chip-Chicken Sticks

Patti Lu Oransky Richboro, PA
Chicken Bayou Petites

Gloria Piantek Nashville, TN
Fiesta Chicken Party Roll

Laura Premo West Palm Beach, FL
Chicken Premo

Sandra E. Rygle Carmichaels, PA
Elegant Chicken Lasagna

Warren Schultz Miami, FL
Chicken Quesadillas

Adele Solazzo Clearwater, FL
Inside-Out Chicken Cordon Bleu

Adele Solazzo Palm Harbor, FL
Chicken-Cheese Pizza Bread

Janet Solomon Ruskin, FL
Chicken Party Pie

Pat Sprankle Nashua, NH
Chicken Boursin En Croûte

Bonnie J. Starr Largo, FL
Savory Chicken Stew

S.H. (Stan) Stewart La Jolla, CA
Mesquite Chicken Fajitas

Karla Vaillancourt Delray Beach, FL
Chicken Casserole Southwestern Style

Ronald J. Weir Milwaukee, WI
Grecian Chicken Breasts

Darol Wetzel Manhattan, MT
Chicken Sandwiches Southwestern Style

Zita Wilensky North Miami, FL
MexaMia Chicken Puffs

INDEX

*Page numbers in **boldface** indicate photographs and illustrations.*

Only Gold Kist Farms® Can Bring You *Simply The Best Chicken*

This limited-edition cookbook comes to you exclusively from the people who know chicken best, Gold Kist Farms. You'll find great recipe ideas for light meals, elegant entertaining, appetizers, and much more in this 160-page book. The collection contains many original recipe creations selected from our files at Gold Kist Farms plus prize-winning recipes from nearly a decade of our Winning Taste Recipe Contest.® This cookbook is sure to become a classic, so order yours today!

SPECIAL MANUFACTURER'S OFFER SIMPLY THE BEST CHICKEN - COOKBOOK OFFER

To celebrate its introduction, Gold Kist Farms® is offering this unique cookbook **valued at $24.95** for only **$15.95** plus shipping. It's a valuable addition to any cookbook library and makes a wonderful gift. Not offered in retail stores, quantities are limited, so please order yours today.

Name ______________________	Quantity ___ X $15.95 ea. = $ _____.__
Address ______________________	Shipping (add $3.50 per book) = $ _____.__
City ______________________	GA residents add $1.36 (7% sales tax) $ _____.__
State ________ ZIP ______________	Enclosed check in amount of: $ _____.__

Personal checks or money orders only. No counter or third-party checks. **Mail check payable to: Gold Kist Inc., Gold Kist Farms Cookbook, PO Box 48369, Atlanta, GA 30301-2210.** ***Please allow 4-6 weeks for delivery. Offer good only within the continental United States.***

SPECIAL MANUFACTURER'S OFFER *SIMPLY THE BEST CHICKEN - COOKBOOK OFFER*

To celebrate its introduction, Gold Kist Farms® is offering this unique cookbook **valued at $24.95** for only **$15.95** plus shipping. It's a valuable addition to any cookbook library and makes a wonderful gift. Not offered in retail stores, quantities are limited, so please order yours today.

Name ______________________________

Address ______________________________

City ______________________________

State ________ ZIP ________________

Quantity ___ X $15.95 ea. = $ _____.__

Shipping (add $3.50 per book) = $ _____.__

GA residents add $1.36 (7% sales tax) $ _____.__

Enclosed check in amount of: $ _____.__

Personal checks or money orders only. No counter or third-party checks. **Mail check payable to: Gold Kist Inc., Gold Kist Farms Cookbook, PO Box 48369, Atlanta, GA 30301-2210.** ***Please allow 4-6 weeks for delivery. Offer good only within the continental United States.***

Only Gold Kist Farms® Can Bring You *Simply The Best Chicken*

This limited-edition cookbook comes to you exclusively from the people who know chicken best, Gold Kist Farms. You'll find great recipe ideas for light meals, elegant entertaining, appetizers, and much more in this 160-page book. The collection contains many original recipe creations selected from our files at Gold Kist Farms plus prize-winning recipes from nearly a decade of our Winning Taste Recipe Contest.® This cookbook is sure to become a classic, so order yours today!